curries

hamlyn
curries

Meg Jansz

Notes

Both metric and imperial measurements have been given in all recipes.
Use one set of measurements only and not a mixture of both.
Standard level spoon measurements are used in all recipes.
1 tablespoon = one 15 ml spoon
1 teaspoon = one 5 ml spoon
Eggs should be medium unless otherwise stated.
Milk should be full fat unless otherwise stated.
Pepper should be freshly ground black pepper unless otherwise stated.
Fresh herbs should be used unless otherwise stated. If unavailable
use dried herbs as an alternative but halve the quantities stated.

Acknowledgements

Art Editor Mark Winwood
Designer Leigh Jones
Commissioning Editor Nicky Hill
Editor Sasha Judelson
Editorial Assistant Kathy Steer
Production Controller Melanie Frantz
Photographer Jeremy Hopley
Home Economist Meg Jansz
Assistant Home Economist Lucy Pitcairn-Knowles
Stylist Helen Trent
Surfaces courtesy of David Wainwright

First published in Great Britain in 1996 by Hamlyn
a division of Octopus Publishing Group Limited
2–4 Heron Quays, London E14 4JP

This paperback edition first published in 2002

ISBN 0 600 60744 5

A CIP catalogue record for this book is available from the British Library
Produced by Toppan, Hong Kong
Printed in China

Contents

A Continent of Spices

Say 'curry' and most of us think of a hot and spicy dish from India, although India is just one of the many Asian countries where exciting combinations of spices are used in everyday cooking. A curry need not be mouth-numbingly hot; it is just as often mild and subtly flavoured. Each region has its own favourite blends of spices, from sweetly fragrant cinnamon, cloves and saffron to fresh scented coriander, lemon grass and lime leaves and tingling hot peppercorns and chillies.

The spicy, savoury dishes that dominate the cuisines of the Indian subcontinent and Southeast Asia are collectively known as curries. The word derives from the Tamil (southern Indian) word *kari*, which means sauce, and the sauces typically made in this part of the world are appetizingly aromatic, redolent of rich blends of spices.

Spices

Spices are dried aromatic parts of plants – including seeds, leaves, bark and roots – whose primary use is as a flavouring. Most spices are grown in tropical countries, but they are thought to have been known in the eastern Mediterranean for at least 5,000 years. So great was the appeal of exotic spices that they were once thought of as a gift worthy of kings and princes, and as such long, hazardous expeditions were undertaken in order to try and obtain spices from countries such as India, China and Indonesia.

In Europe, spices remained an expensive luxury, while in their native lands they were used in everyday cooking, each region using them in slightly different ways, and combining them with fresh herbs, local vegetables, nuts and fruit and meat or fish. Thus, although it is possible to describe all these spicy dishes as curries, there are actually subtle differences between the curries of India and those of Sri Lanka, Thailand and Indonesia. These differences may not strike you immediately but on a second or third tasting they will more than likely do so.

The cuisines of Asia

The *Pocket Oxford Dictionary* defines curry as 'a dish of meat etc. cooked with curry powder and usually served with rice' – an uninspiring description of the evocative aromas and flavours found in Asian cooking. 'Meat etc.' seems a rather dull way to summarize the main ingredients of curries, which may equally well be made with fish, shellfish, exotic vegetables and tropical fruits and nuts. 'Curry powder' is not a standard blend, but is almost infinitely variable (it may include a dozen or more spices) and the basis for a curry is just as likely to be a paste in which the spices are blended with fresh herbs and other moist ingredients. And while it is true that rice is the usual accompaniment to curries, breads or noodles are traditional in some regions.

In Britain, many people's first experience was of Indian curries – or sometimes rather strange and distant derivations of them – but Thai, Indonesian and Malaysian curries are now widely enjoyed, as are curries from other Asian countries.

My own interest in curries comes from several different influences: I grew up in Malaysia and have travelled extensively throughout Asia and have researched the many regional differences in food while I have been there, some of my ancestors are from Sri Lanka and my work is food. I adore the continent of Asia and Asian food. There are so many varieties of food available and so many different combinations. Something to please and satisfy everyone. I was educated in the United Kingdom and have found it fascinating to see how people's attitude to food, and curries in particular, has changed over the years.

Curries are no longer thought of only as 'hot' and to be eaten anywhere but not at home. They are a delicious example of the many different flavours that come out of the continent of Asia, how the culture and lifestyles influence the population, and how people make the most of their local food resources.

In this book I have divided up most of the curries according to their country of origin, but in the first two chapters – Soups, starters and snacks, and Fast and simple curries – I have drawn inspiration from far and wide. Spiced Nuts (see page 21) uses an Indian spice blend to create a simply prepared snack that makes a great pre-dinner nibble. The flavours of Thailand appear in the elegant, if more time-consuming, Chillies Stuffed with Curried Crab (see page 18).

These chapters also show how to make the most of commercially prepared curry pastes and powders, often combining them with everyday storecupboard ingredients, yet producing authentic Asian curries. Cooks who are in a hurry can choose a fiery Thai Red Beef Curry (see page 32), a mild, rich Prawn and Mango Curry (see page 33) or simply vary the 'heat' of a recipe by adjusting the amount of chilli. Don't be afraid to experiment and see which curries suit your particular taste and that of your family and guests, the recipe variations also give you an opportunity to experiment.

The Indian subcontinent

This huge area – divided from the rest of Asia by the Himalayas – is roughly the same size as all the countries of Europe put together, so it is not surprising that each region has its own traditions, based on climate and soil. Coastal areas have some very fine seafood, which is completely inaccessible inland. Added to the regional variety is the influence of the many religions and sects: some Hindus are strictly vegetarian, and none will eat beef; the Muslims will not eat pork; the state of Kerala in the southwest has had a thriving Christian community since the 1st century AD; and the Parsee and Bohri religions are among those that have developed their own cuisines. Outside influences on Indian taste have, throughout history, come from Persia, Portugal and Britain, but Indians have fortunately never lost their skill in using and blending spices. (One of the most important additions to the language of curries came comparatively late in history, when the Portuguese introduced chilli peppers from the New World in the 16th century.)

I have chosen Indian curry recipes from different corners of the subcontinent: there is a Kerala Prawn Curry from the south (see page 48), which uses plenty of chillies in combination with coconut milk; a Kashmir Kofta Curry from the north (see page 57), in which spiced meatballs are simmered in yogurt sauce; and a Lamb and Pork Curry from Goa in the west (see page 61), typical of the region in its use of vinegar.

Sri Lanka is, of course, part of the subcontinent, but a separate chapter has been devoted to this island, so that you can taste the difference in typical Sri Lankan curries, which are made with a dark-roasted spice mixture. See page 12 for an explanation of dark-roasting and the flavours that this cooking technique gives.

Thailand, Burma and Indochina

The particular aromas and flavours of curries from these countries are created by the addition of pungent kaffir lime leaves and fragrant lemon grass, two ingredients rarely used in the Indian subcontinent. The curries often require less cooking than their rich, slow-cooked Indian counterparts – most of the time is spent in the preparation, not the cooking. A good example is the Siamese Pineapple and Mussel Curry (see page 72).

The Burmese Chicken Curry with Cellophane Noodles (see page 78) is typical of the traditional cuisine of Burma, in that it is served with lots of accompaniments, so that each diner can make their own curry hotter or cooler, more tangy or more crunchy.

The cooking of Indochina (which includes the countries of Laos, Cambodia and Vietnam) has its own interpretations of both curries and Chinese cooking. I have selected just a few typical dishes, such as the Cambodian Prawn and Marrow Curry (see page 74), which has a distinctive flavour from the use of fennel seeds.

Malaysia and Indonesia

Coconut milk, peanuts, tamarind, shrimp paste and chillies are all important flavours in the curries of these countries, which lie either side of the Equator. They have always been receptive to the influences of outside traders, particularly the Chinese, and ingredients such as soy sauce and bean sprouts are found, most notably in the distinctive cuisine of the Nonyas of Malaysia – descendants of Chinese traders who settled in coastal areas.

Side dishes

No curry is complete without some sort of accompaniment and rice, the staple food in nearly all curry-eating countries. It is ideal for absorbing the tasty sauce that comes with the main dish. It does not always have to be plain, boiled and white. I have included a selection of more elaborate rice dishes such as Sri Lankan Yellow Rice (see page 102) and Nasi Minyak, a fragrant spiced rice from Malaysia (see page 101), which complement the cuisines of their countries of origin.

In northern India the staple grain is wheat, and Indian cooks have devised a number of interesting breads, from the simple Chapati (see page 109) to Kulcha, which can be stuffed with a delicious cooked onion mixture (see page 100).

Other accompaniments include a quick and unusual yogurt-based Papaya and Coriander Raita

(see page 108), fruity chutneys and tangy pickles, which keep very well and can be made in larger quantities and stored for 2–3 months.

In the kitchen

As I hope this book will show, it is not difficult to make authentic-tasting curries now that so many spices and exotic herbs such as lemon grass are increasingly widely available. Before you begin, I would like to share some simple tips for making perfect curries.

Roasting and grinding spices

It is nice to make one's own curry powders and pastes when time permits: they can be kept for days, weeks or months, depending on the ingredients (see pages 115–118).

It is usually best to begin with whole spices and to heat them briefly to release their aromatic oils. This can be done in an oven or under a grill, but the most reliable way is to dry-roast or dry-fry them in a pan on top of the hob. A heavy-based pan allows gentle, even heat, and 1–4 minutes is usually long enough for the spices to become fragrant. Some curry bases require slightly longer cooking, particularly if the spices need to be lightly coloured or darker still, as in the typical curry powders of Sri Lanka.

The dry-roasted spices should be left to cool, then ground to a powder. This can be done with a pestle and mortar, in a hand-turned spice mill or coffee grinder, (be sure to wipe away all trace of spices with kitchen paper before grinding coffee) or an electric grinder. If the quantity of spices is large enough, a blender or food processor can be used. For moist curry pastes it is best to use a blender or food processor.

However, if time is short one can always use shop-bought equivalents found in most Asian grocers and in some supermarkets. Most ready-made products which are available nowadays are good and authentic.

Ghee and cooking oils

The clarified butter known as ghee was first developed in northern India, quite possibly by nomadic peoples who had no regular crops of oil-rich seeds or nuts, but needed an easily transportable cooking fat. Because it was thoroughly clarified (all the milk solids were removed) it did not need to be refrigerated and could be heated to high temperatures without burning. Ghee has a distinctively rich, nutty flavour and is used in northern Indian curries and rice dishes. It is also used in Sri Lankan curries. Ghee is available from some supermarkets and Indian shops where it is sold in tins and keeps for 2–3 months in the refrigerator.

In other parts of Asia cooking oils have traditionally been pressed from various seeds and nuts. Almost any neutral-flavoured vegetable oil can be used when cooking curries. Sunflower oil is a good all-purpose oil, and groundnut oil is favoured for curries from Thailand, Malaysia and Indonesia. All are readily available in most supermarkets.

Mustard oil is used all over India, but particularly in the north and east. When raw it has quite a pungent taste, but when heated it has a sweet fragrance and it is very good in lentil curries or dhals. It is available from Indian shops.

Yogurt

Yogurt is frequently used to add a tart creaminess to Indian curries. Always use natural yogurt, preferably a thin, sharp-flavoured variety rather than the more creamy Greek or Bio yogurts. If it is a 'set' yogurt always mix to break the 'setting' before adding it to the curry or before serving it as an accompaniment.

Acidity

Acidity is often used to balance or enhance the flavours of curries. It may be added early or late in the cooking process through a number of ingredients, including tamarind, vinegar, tomatoes, lemon or lime juice. These naturally acidic ingredients can also act as a meat tenderiser or, when used in fairly large amounts, for example in Duck Vindaloo (see page 52), as a preservative. You do not need to worry about these ingredients giving your curry a really sour taste: they will not. If you are worried try adding ingredients like vinegar and lemon or

lime juice gradually, and taste after each addition until you achieve the balance of flavours which suits your tastes.

Sweetness

Sugar is added to many curries to act as a flavour enhancer and to 'balance' the flavours. It is generally added towards the end of the cooking time. White or brown sugar may be used, and palm sugar (a product of the coconut palm tree) is a common sweetener in Thailand. It is available in brown 'cakes' from Thai grocers, but if it is unavailable, you can use soft brown sugar instead.

Seasoning

Seasoning a curry can be slightly different from what we normally think of as seasoning. Curries do not usually use pepper as a seasoning but rather salt and, in Thai dishes, they will use fish sauce. In this book where I have referred to the amount of seasoning, this means either salt or fish sauce, whichever is used in the recipe. Do not try using pepper unless it is ;isted in the ingredients.

I have enjoyed writing and cooking for this book enormously, and I hope that you have fun making the recipes on the following pages.

Soups,
Starters
and
Snacks

The use of curry spices adds an extra
dimension to first-course dishes: their
rich aromas and flavours are very
satisfying, and many of the soups and
snacks in this chapter make a one-dish
meal in themselves. The laden tables of
traditional banquets contribute more
delicate starters, each one designed first
to catch the eye and then to whet the
appetite in one or two mouthfuls.

Puris with Curried Fish

Puris – cushions of deep-fried bread – can be made with wholemeal flour, which produces a 'nutty' flavour, or plain flour, which produces a lighter, airy texture. It is illustrated on pages 14–15.

1 Heat the oil in a heavy-based saucepan, add the onion and garlic and fry over a gentle heat, stirring, for about 5 minutes until softened. Stir in the cumin, sesame and mustard seeds and the curry paste and fry for 2 minutes.

2 Stir in the garam masala and turmeric and fry for 1 minute. Add the tomato purée, diced tomatoes, salt and 75 ml/3 fl oz water to the pan. Stir well, cover and simmer gently for about 10 minutes.

3 Gently stir the fish into the curry sauce and cook, covered, for 7–8 minutes until the fish is just cooked. Stir in the coriander, taking care not to break up the fish too much. Add salt, if necessary. Serve the curry hot with plain or spiced puris.

4 To make the puris, place the flour and the salt in a large mixing bowl. Add the oil and lightly rub it into the flour with your fingertips until the mixture resembles breadcrumbs.

Curried Fish:

3 tablespoons vegetable oil

1 onion, chopped

2 garlic cloves, crushed

1 teaspoon cumin seeds

½ teaspoon sesame seeds

½ teaspoon mustard seeds

2 tablespoons mild curry paste

1 teaspoon garam masala (see page 117)

½ teaspoon turmeric

1 tablespoon tomato purée

3 tomatoes, peeled and diced

½ teaspoon salt

500 g/1 lb skinless, boneless halibut or cod, cut into 1 cm/½ inch cubes

2 tablespoons torn fresh coriander leaves

Puris:

250 g/8 oz wholemeal or plain flour

½ teaspoon salt

2 tablespoons vegetable oil

vegetable oil for deep-frying

Add 125 ml/4 fl oz warm water and work it in to produce a firm dough.

5 Knead the dough on a floured surface for about 2 minutes or until it is smooth. Divide the dough into 18–20 balls. Roll out a dough ball on a floured surface to produce a thin 10 cm/4 inch circle. (Keep the dough covered with a damp cloth when not working so it does not dry out.)

3 Heat the oil for deep-frying to 180–190°C (350–375°F), or until a cube of bread browns in 30 seconds. Cook 2 puris at a time in very hot oil for 30 seconds on each side. They will puff up and go golden. Remove them with a slotted spoon and drain on absorbent kitchen paper. Serve the hot, freshly cooked puris with the curried fish.

- Serves 4–6
- Preparation time: 40 minutes
- Cooking time: 20 minutes

Curried Chicken and Peanut Soup

I Soak the shiitake mushrooms in cold water for 30 minutes, then drain and slice thickly. Set them aside.

2 In a pestle and mortar, combine the garlic cloves with the black peppercorns, to form a paste. Heat the groundnut oil in a saucepan, add the garlic and pepper paste and the Thai green curry paste. Fry over a gentle heat for 3 minutes, stirring occasionally.

3 Add the chicken. Fry for a further 2 minutes.

4 Stir in the chicken stock, peanuts and mushrooms, and then cook gently for a further 10 minutes.

5 Add the spring onions, coriander and fish sauce. Heat gently for 2 minutes, taste and add more fish sauce, if necessary. Serve the soup immediately.

- Serves 4–6
- Preparation time: 10 minutes plus 30 minutes soaking time
- Cooking time: 20 minutes

5 dried shiitake mushrooms

2 garlic cloves, crushed

½ teaspoon black peppercorns

I tablespoon groundnut oil

I tablespoon Thai green curry paste (see page 118)

I skinless, boneless chicken breast, cut diagonally into thin strips

1.2 litres/2 pints chicken stock

50 g/2 oz skinless raw peanuts

4 spring onions, cut on the diagonal

2 tablespoons chopped fresh coriander

I tablespoon fish sauce

Variation

Thai-style Curried Vermicelli Soup

Try using different noodles in this soup like thin egg noodles or rice sticks. Follow the cooking instructions on the packet, then add to the soup as suggested in the recipe.

I Heat 2 tablespoons of groundnut oil in a large saucepan, add 2 shallots, chopped, 1 stalk of lemon grass, very finely chopped, 2 Kaffir lime leaves, finely chopped, 3 garlic cloves, crushed, and 1 green chilli, deseeded and sliced, and cook over a low heat, stirring occasionally, for 4 minutes.

2 Stir in 1 tablespoon Thai red curry paste (see page 118) and 1.2 litres/2 pints chicken stock, bring to the boil, then reduce the heat and simmer gently for 15 minutes.

3 Meanwhile soak 125 g/4 oz clear vermicelli in boiling water for 5 minutes, drain and then add the cooked vermicelli to the saucepan together with 2 teaspoons of fish sauce and 1 teaspoon soft brown sugar. Simmer the soup gently for a further 4 minutes.

4 Stir 3 tablespoons of torn fresh coriander leaves into the hot soup, add more fish sauce, if necessary. Ladle the soup into warm serving bowls and serve immediately.

- Serves 4
- Preparation time: 10 minutes
- Cooking time: 25 minutes

Thai-style Curried Chicken Skewers

If you are using wooden skewers, soak them in cold water for 30 minutes before using them to prevent them from burning during cooking.

1 Place the ingredients for the curry marinade in a non-metallic bowl and mix well to combine. Add the chicken pieces to the marinade and turn them to ensure they are evenly coated. If time allows, cover the bowl and leave to marinate in the refrigerator for 2 hours.

2 Thread the marinated chicken on to 8 metal or wooden skewers, alternating them with the pepper chunks. Reserve any remaining marinade.

3 Cook the chicken skewers under a preheated medium hot grill for about 7 minutes on each side, basting them with the reserved marinade whilst they are cooking.

4 Serve the chicken at once, garnished with lime wedges and coriander sprigs.

- Serves 4
- Preparation time: about 30 minutes, plus 2 hours marinating (optional)
- Cooking time: about 7 minutes

500 g/1 lb skinless, boneless chicken breasts or thighs, cut into 2.5 cm/1 inch pieces

small green pepper, cored and cut into 16 chunks

To garnish:

lime wedges

coriander sprigs, to garnish

Curry Marinade:

2 tablespoons Thai red curry paste (see page 118) or use a shop-bought variety

1 tablespoon ground coriander

2 tablespoons chopped fresh coriander

3 tablespoons groundnut oil

1 tablespoon ground cumin

2 teaspoons soft brown sugar

1 stalk lemon grass, very finely chopped

juice of 2 limes

Chillies Stuffed with Curried Crab

Use jalapeño chillies for this recipe as they have thicker flesh than some chillies, making them easier to peel and stuff. This delicious recipe is illustrated opposite.

1 Prepare the chillies for stuffing. Place them under a preheated hot grill and cook them, turning occasionally until they have softened and their skins are patched with black. This will take about 8–10 minutes.

2 Remove the chillies from the grill and leave them to cool, covered with sheets of dampened kitchen paper. (This will make them easier to peel once they have cooled.)

3 Meanwhile prepare the stuffing. Heat the oil in a saucepan, add the garlic, ginger and spring onions and cook over a gentle heat for 3 minutes until softened. Stir in the lime leaves, red curry paste and turmeric and cook, stirring, for a further 2 minutes. Remove the pan from the heat and stir in the flaked crab, lime juice and fish sauce.

4 Peel the chillies, leaving the stalks intact and make a slit down one side of each chilli from the stalk to the tip. Scrape out and discard the seeds. Stuff the chillies with the curried crab mixture and place them in a shallow ovenproof dish and cover them with foil.

5 Just before serving, place the chillies in a preheated oven, 200°C (400°F), Gas Mark 6, for 15 minutes, until they are heated through. Serve immediately.

- Serves 4–6
- Preparation time: about 30 minutes
- Cooking time: 30 minutes

6 red jalapeño chillies

6 green jalapeño chillies

2 tablespoons vegetable oil

2 garlic cloves, crushed

1 teaspoon grated fresh root ginger

3 spring onions, chopped

2 Kaffir lime leaves, very finely chopped

1 tablespoon Thai red curry paste (see page 118)

¼ teaspoon turmeric

150 g/5 oz fresh or canned white crab meat, flaked

1 tablespoon lime juice

2 teaspoons fish sauce

18

Sour Curried Seafood Soup

1 Soak the tamarind pulp in 150 ml/¼ pint boiling water for 10 minutes, then strain the pulp through a sieve pressing it against the sieve to extract as much tamarind flavour as possible. Discard the pulp and reserve the liquid.

2 Heat the oil in a saucepan, add the onion, garlic and ginger and fry over a gentle heat, stirring, for about 5 minutes until softened but not coloured.

3 Add the ground coriander, cumin, turmeric, chilli powder, mustard seeds, fenugreek and curry paste and cook gently, stirring, for a further 2 minutes.

4 Add the fish stock and reserved tamarind liquid, stir well, then simmer gently for 10 minutes. Add the tomatoes, salt and lemon juice and simmer for a further 4 minutes .

5 Stir the fish into the soup and cook gently for 4 minutes, until the fish is just cooked. Add the prawns and the chopped coriander and heat through gently for 2 minutes. Taste and add a little more salt, if necessary, and serve the soup immediately.

- Serves 4–6
- Preparation time: about 20 minutes
- Cooking time: 30 minutes

1 tablespoon tamarind pulp

3 tablespoons vegetable oil

1 onion, finely chopped

2 garlic cloves, crushed

2.5 cm/1 inch piece of fresh root ginger, grated

2 teaspoons ground coriander

2 teaspoons ground cumin

1 teaspoon turmeric

1 teaspoon chilli powder

½ teaspoon black mustard seeds

¼ teaspoon ground fenugreek

2 teaspoons Madras curry paste (see page 117)

1 litre/1¾ pints fish stock

3 tomatoes, cut into wedges

1 teaspoon salt

1 tablespoon lemon juice

250 g/8 oz skinless halibut fillets, cut into bite-sized pieces

125 g/4 oz cooked peeled prawns

2 tablespoons chopped fresh coriander

Mushrooms Stuffed with Curried Pork

1 Remove the stalks from the mushrooms and chop the stalks finely, ready for use in the stuffing. Heat 1 tablespoon of the oil in a heavy-based frying pan, add the onion, garlic and ginger and cook over a gentle heat, stirring occasionally, for 4 minutes or until softened. Add the chopped mushroom stalks and curry paste and cook, stirring, for a further 2 minutes.

2 Stir in the minced pork and mix well so it is evenly coated with the fried mixture. Cook over a gentle heat, stirring frequently, for about 10 minutes. Stir in the carrot, peas and salt and cook for a further 5 minutes. Taste and add a little more salt, if necessary.

3 Brush the base of each mushroom with a little of the remaining oil and divide the curried pork mixture between the mushrooms. Place them in a shallow, ovenproof dish, cover with foil and bake in a preheated oven, 180°C (350°F), Gas Mark 4, for 15–20 minutes until the mushrooms are tender and the filling is heated through. Serve immediately, with a few toasted sesame seeds scattered over each mushroom.

- Serves 4
- Preparation time: about 15 minutes
- Cooking time: 30–45 minutes

8 flat mushrooms weighing about 50 g/2 oz each

3 tablespoons vegetable oil

1 small onion, finely chopped

2 garlic cloves, crushed

2 teaspoons grated fresh root ginger

2 tablespoons Madras curry paste (see page 117)

250 g/8 oz minced pork

1 small carrot, coarsely grated

50 g/2 oz frozen peas, defrosted

¼ teaspoon salt

toasted sesame seeds, to garnish

Spiced Curried Nuts

1 Heat the oil in a large heavy-based frying pan. Add all the nuts and the sesame seeds and sunflower seeds and cook over a gentle heat, stirring frequently for about 8–10 minutes until the nuts are a light golden brown all over.

2 Add the curry powder and chilli powder to the pan and mix well to coat the nuts evenly in the spices. Cook, stirring frequently, for a further 2 minutes until the nuts are fragrant.

3 Tip the cooked nuts into a large bowl, stir in the sugar and season generously with sea salt. Leave to cool completely, then store in an airtight container and use as required.

3 tablespoons vegetable oil

125 g/4 oz raw cashew nuts

125 g/4 oz blanched almonds

125 g/4 oz skinless raw peanuts

2 tablespoons sesame seeds

2 tablespoons sunflower seeds

1 tablespoon basic Indian curry powder (see page 116)

1 teaspoon chilli powder

¼ teaspoon caster sugar

sea salt

- Serves 6–8
- Preparation time: 5 minutes
- Cooking time: 15 minutes

Stuffed Curried Eggs

1 Heat the oil in a saucepan, add the garlic, shallots, chilli, ginger and the green curry paste and cook over a gentle heat, stirring frequently, for 5 minutes. Set aside to cool.

2 Shell the eggs and cut them in half lengthways. Scoop out the yolks and reserve the yolks from 3 of the eggs for the filling. (The remaining yolks can be sieved and used as a garnish with the lettuce, if desired.)

3 Place the garlic and shallot mixture in a food processor or blender and add the fish sauce, torn coriander, prawns and the 3 egg yolks. Process briefly until all the ingredients are evenly combined, but do not allow the mixture to become too pulpy. Divide the curried prawn mixture between the 12 egg white halves.

4 Garnish the stuffed eggs with the chopped chilli and coriander sprigs and serve on a bed of Cos lettuce leaves.

2 tablespoons vegetable oil

2 garlic cloves, crushed

2 shallots, finely chopped

2 teaspoons chopped fresh red chilli

2 teaspoons grated fresh root ginger

1 tablespoon Thai green curry paste (see page 118)

6 hard-boiled eggs

2 teaspoons fish sauce

2 tablespoons torn fresh coriander leaves

125 g/4 oz cooked peeled prawns

To garnish:

1 fresh red chilli, chopped

sprigs of coriander

Cos lettuce leaves

- Serves 6
- Preparation time: about 25 minutes
- Cooking time: 5 minutes

21

Steamed Masala Mussels

This delicious recipe is illustrated opposite.

1 Scrub the mussels with a stiff brush and use a small, sharp knife to scrape off the beard and any barnacles. Wash well in cold water and discard any open mussels.

2 Heat the oil in a large deep saucepan, add the onions, garlic, ginger and chillies and cook over a gentle heat, stirring occasionally, for 5 minutes or until softened. Stir in the saffron with its water, the ground coriander and cumin and cook for a further 1 minute.

3 Add the salt and 300 ml/½ pint water to the pan, then stir in the mussels, cover the pan and cook for about 5–6 minutes or until all the mussels have opened and cooked through. Discard any mussels that have not opened. Stir the lime juice and chopped coriander into the pan, taste and adjust the seasoning, if necessary.

4 Ladle the hot mussels and the masala sauce into 4 deep bowls and garnish each portion with a sprig of fresh coriander if you wish. Serve immediately.

1.5 kg/3 lb fresh mussels

3 tablespoons groundnut oil

2 red onions, very finely chopped

4 garlic cloves, crushed

2 tablespoons grated fresh root ginger

3 large green chillies, deseeded and finely chopped

¼ teaspoon saffron threads infused in 2 tablespoons boiling water for 10 minutes

2 teaspoons ground coriander

2 teaspoons ground cumin

½ teaspoon salt

2 tablespoons lime juice

4 tablespoons chopped fresh coriander

a few sprigs of coriander, to garnish (optional)

- Serves 4
- Preparation time: about 40 minutes
- Cooking time: 10–15 minutes

Mulligatawny Soup

The meeting of East with West in the 300 years of the British Raj produced Anglo-Indian dishes such as this soup. The name Mulligatawny derives from the Tamil for 'pepper water'.

1 Place all the ingredients for the beef stock in a large, deep saucepan, pour over 1.5 litres/2½ pints water and bring to the boil. Then lower the heat and simmer the stock gently, uncovered, for 1 hour to allow the liquid to reduce slightly. After 1 hour cover the pan and cook the stock for a further 45 minutes, until the stewing steak is very tender. Remove the steak and set aside to cool.

2 Strain the stock through a fine sieve, discard the bones and spices and reserve the stock until required. Once the steak has cooled, dice it finely.

3 Place the dried chillies, cumin, fennel, saffron and mustard seeds in a heavy-based frying pan over a gentle heat and cook, stirring constantly for 2 minutes, or until they are fragrant, then place them in a spice mill and grind to a powder or crush them finely, using a pestle and mortar.

4 Heat the oil in a heavy-based saucepan, add the onion and fry, stirring occasionally, for 10–12 minutes until it is soft and golden. Add the ground spices and the curry leaves and cook for 2 minutes. Add the reserved stock, stir to mix, bring to the boil then reduce the heat and simmer for 5 minutes.

4 dried red chillies
¼ teaspoon cumin seeds
¼ teaspoon fennel seeds
¼ teaspoon saffron threads
½ teaspoon black mustard seeds
1 tablespoon vegetable oil
1 large onion, sliced
5 curry leaves
200 ml/7 fl oz coconut milk
juice of 1 lime
Beef Stock:
500 g/1 lb stewing steak in 1 piece
1 kg/2 lb beef bones for soup
5 curry leaves
1 tablespoon coriander seeds, lightly crushed
2 teaspoons cumin seeds, lightly crushed
4 cardamom pods, bruised
4 garlic cloves, halved
1 onion studded with 4 cloves
1 tablespoon lime juice
1 teaspoon salt
¼ teaspoon black peppercorns

5 Stir in the coconut milk, diced steak and lime juice and heat the soup through for 3 minutes without allowing it to boil. Taste and add a little more salt, if necessary, and serve the hot soup immediately.

- Serves 4–6
- Preparation time: 20 minutes
- Cooking time: 2¼ hours

Beef and Potato Curry Puffs

1 Start by making the filling. Heat the vegetable oil in a heavy-based frying pan, add the onion, garlic, ginger and chilli and fry over a gentle heat, stirring constantly, for about 5 minutes until softened. Stir in the curry paste and fry for about 1 minute, until fragrant.

2 Stir in the minced beef and salt, mix well and fry for 5 minutes, stirring occasionally. Stir in the diced potato and cook for a further 2 minutes. Taste and add more salt, if necessary, and leave the beef filling to cool.

3 Roll out the pastry thinly on a lightly floured surface. Using a pastry cutter, stamp out 24 x 10 cm/4 inch circles and place 1 heaped teaspoon of beef filling on one half of each circle. Dampen the edges of the pastry with water and fold over to produce a semi-circle. Press together to seal the edges.

4 Heat the oil in a saucepan for deep-frying. Deep-fry the curry puffs in batches, allowing 5–6 minutes for each batch, and turning halfway through, until they are crisp and golden. (Do not allow the oil to get too hot or the pastry will burn.) Remove with a slotted spoon and drain on kitchen paper. Leave to cool slightly and serve warm or cold, if preferred.

- Makes 24
- Preparation time: about 35–40 minutes plus pastry-making time
- Cooking time: 20–25 minutes

1 tablespoon vegetable oil

1 small onion, finely chopped

2 garlic cloves, crushed

1 teaspoon grated fresh root ginger

1 small fresh red chilli, deseeded and chopped finely

2 tablespoons medium curry paste

250 g/8 oz minced beef

½ teaspoon salt

175 g/6 oz cooked potato, finely diced

625 g/1¼ lb shortcrust pastry

oil for deep-frying

Variation

Chicken, Coriander and Sweet Potato Curry Puffs

1 To make the filling, heat 2 tablespoons of groundnut oil in a heavy-based frying pan, add 4 spring onions, chopped, 2 garlic cloves, crushed, and 1 green chilli, deseeded and chopped, and fry for 3 minutes, stirring frequently.

2 Stir in 2 teaspoons each of ground coriander and cumin, 1 teaspoon ground turmeric and 1 tablespoon medium curry paste and fry for 2 minutes.

3 Stir in 250 g/8 oz skinless, boneless chicken breast, finely chopped, and cook, stirring, for 5 minutes. Stir in 25 g/1 oz creamed coconut dissolved in 75 ml/3 fl oz boiling water, 2 tablespoons chopped fresh coriander and ¼ teaspoon salt and cook, stirring, for a further 5 minutes. Stir in 125 g/4 oz cooked and mashed sweet potato and heat through for just 1 minute. Taste and a little more salt, if necessary and allow the filling to cool before making into the curry puffs.

4 Use 625 g/1¼ lb shortcrust pastry and prepare and fry the curry puffs as described in the main recipe. Serve the puffs warm or cold.

- Makes 24
- Preparation time: about 35–40 minutes plus pastry-making time
- Cooking time: 20–25 minutes

25

Prawns Steamed in Banana Leaves

1 Place the garlic, shallot, galangal, lemon grass, Kaffir lime leaves, chilli flakes, chilli oil, fish sauce, lime juice and sugar in a food processor or blender and blend to produce a thick paste. Place the creamed coconut in a bowl and pour over 75 ml/3 fl oz boiling water. Stir to dissolve the coconut, then add the coconut milk to the spice paste. Mix well.

2 Place the prawns in a bowl and add the coconut spice mixture. Stir to coat the prawns evenly. Lay the 4 pieces of banana leaf on a flat surface (or use buttered greaseproof paper if banana leaves are unavailable). Place 6 prawns and a quarter of the coconut mixture in the centre of each leaf. Wrap up the leaves to enclose the prawns, forming neat parcels.

3 Steam the prawn parcels in a steamer over boiling water for 8–10 minutes.

4 To serve, remove the prawns from the leaves and place on 4 serving plates. Pour the coconut sauce into a bowl and whisk briefly until smooth. Pour a little sauce over each portion, garnish with spring onions, and serve immediately.

2 garlic cloves, chopped

1 shallot, chopped

5 cm/2 inch piece of fresh galangal, peeled and chopped

1 stalk of lemon grass, finely chopped

3 Kaffir lime leaves, chopped

1 teaspoon dried red chilli flakes

2 teaspoons chilli oil

1 tablespoon fish sauce

1 tablespoon lime juice

¼ teaspoon caster sugar

25 g/1 oz creamed coconut, chopped

24 uncooked prawns, peeled with tails left intact

4 large pieces of banana leaf (see method)

sliced spring onions, to garnish (optional)

- Serves 4
- Preparation time: about 20 minutes
- Cooking time: 20 minutes

Curried Sweetcorn Patties

These patties are an ideal starter for a dinner party or eaten as a light lunch snack. They are illustrated opposite.

1 Reserve 4 tablespoons of the sweetcorn. Place the remaining corn in a food processor or blender with the cornflour, plain flour, egg, salt, curry powder, chilli powder and turmeric. Blend briefly to combine the ingredients (the corn should be slightly broken up) then transfer the mixture to a bowl and stir in the shallot, coriander and reserved sweetcorn.

2 Heat the oil in a saucepan for deep-frying to 180–190°C (350–375°F), or until a cube of bread browns in 30 seconds. Drop dessertspoonfuls of the corn mixture into the hot oil and cook the patties in batches for 3–4 minutes per batch until they are crisp and golden. Remove with a slotted spoon and drain on kitchen paper.

3 Mix together all the ingredients for the yogurt dip, taste and adjust the seasoning if necessary. Serve hot, with the yogurt dip, garnished with the lemon wedges and coriander.

375 g/12 oz sweetcorn kernels

2 tablespoons cornflour, sieved

2 tablespoons plain flour, sieved

1 egg, beaten lightly

¼ teaspoon salt

1 teaspoon basic Indian curry powder (see page 116)

½ teaspoon chilli powder

¼ teaspoon turmeric

1 shallot, very finely chopped

2 tablespoons chopped fresh coriander

oil for deep-frying

Yogurt Dip:

4 tablespoons natural yogurt

1 tablespoon lemon juice

1 tablespoon chopped fresh coriander

1 teaspoon clear honey

¼ teaspoon garam masala (see page 117)

¼ teaspoon salt

To garnish:

lemon wedges

a few sprigs of coriander

- Makes about 20 patties
- Preparation time: 20–30 minutes
- Cooking time: 15 minutes

Vegetable Samosas

1 Cook the carrots and potatoes in separate pans of boiling, salted water until they are tender. The potatoes will take about 8 minutes and the carrots about 7 minutes. Add the sliced beans to the pan of carrots after 4–5 minutes. Drain the cooked vegetables and set them aside.

2 Heat the oil in a heavy-based frying pan, add the shallots and garlic and then fry, stirring frequently, for 5 minutes or until softened. Stir in the curry paste and mango chutney and cook for 1 minute.

3 Stir in the cooked vegetables together with the peas, coriander and salt and then cook for a further 2 minutes. Taste and add more salt, if necessary, and then leave the filling to cool before making the samosas.

4 Cut the filo pastry into 20 strips, each measuring 10 cm/4 inches by 30 cm/12 inches. Divide the filling into 10 portions. Place 2 strips of filo pastry on top of each other and place a portion of filling at one end. (Keep the filo strips covered with a damp cloth to prevent them from drying out.)

125 g/4 oz carrots, peeled and finely diced

125 g/4 oz potatoes, peeled and finely diced

50 g/2 oz green beans, finely sliced

2 tablespoons vegetable oil

2 shallots, finely chopped

2 garlic cloves, crushed

2 tablespoons hot curry paste

2 tablespoons mango chutney

50 g/2 oz frozen peas, defrosted

2 tablespoons chopped fresh coriander

¼ teaspoon salt

250 g/8 oz filo pastry

vegetable oil for deep-frying

Carefully fold a corner of the pastry over to the opposite edge to form a triangle enclosing the filling, then continue folding triangles along the strip. Seal the edges with a little water. Repeat with the remaining pastry and filling to form 10 samosas.

5 Heat the oil in a saucepan for deep-frying to 180–190°C (350–375°F), or until a cube of bread browns in 30 seconds. Fry the samosas in 3 batches allowing 5 minutes for each batch, or until they are crisp and golden. Remove with a slotted spoon and drain on absorbent kitchen paper. Serve them hot or cold.

- Makes 10
- Preparation time: about 30 minutes
- Cooking time: 30 minutes

Variation

Spicy Beef and Ginger Samosas

1 To make the filling, heat 2 tablespoons of vegetable oil in a heavy-based frying pan, add 2 shallots, chopped, 2 garlic cloves, crushed, and 1 tablespoon grated fresh root ginger. Fry, stirring frequently, for 5 minutes until softened.
2 Stir in 1 teaspoon black mustard seeds, 2 tablespoons Madras curry paste (see page 117) and 2 teaspoons garam masala (see page 117) and fry for 2 minutes. Stir in 250 g/ 8 oz lean minced beef, 2 tablespoons tomato purée and ½ teaspoon salt and cook, stirring occasionally, for 10 minutes.
3 Add 50 g/2 oz frozen peas, defrosted, and 2 tablespoons chopped fresh coriander to the pan and cook for a further 2 minutes. Taste and adjust the seasoning if necessary, then leave the filling to cool before making the samosas.
4 Use 250 g/8 oz filo pastry to make the samosas and prepare and fry the samosas as described in the main recipe. Serve the samosas hot or cold.

- Makes 10
- Preparation time: about 30 minutes
- Cooking time: 35–40 minutes

Curried Vegetable and Coconut Soup

1 Heat the oil in a saucepan and add the shallots and garlic. Cook over a gentle heat for 4 minutes, or until softened. Add the curry powder and ground black pepper and cook for a further 1 minute.
2 Add the stock and bring it to boiling point. Stir in the bok choy, bean sprouts, sweetcorn, spring onions and rice and season with salt to taste. Lower the heat and simmer the soup for 5 minutes or until all the vegetables are just tender.
3 Stir the coconut milk into the soup and heat it through gently, without letting the soup boil. Taste and adjust the seasoning, if necessary.
4 Ladle the soup into warm serving bowls and garnish with chilli rings, sliced shallot and coriander leaves. Serve the soup immediately.

3 tablespoons groundnut oil
3 shallots, thinly sliced
2 garlic cloves, crushed
1½ tablespoons medium hot curry powder
¼ teaspoon ground black pepper
1.2 litres/2 pints vegetable stock
125 g/4 oz bok choy or kai choy, (mustard cabbage) shredded coarsely
125 g/4 oz bean sprouts
4 baby sweetcorn, halved lengthways
4 spring onions, sliced diagonally
175 g/6 oz cooked white rice
150 ml/¼ pint coconut milk
salt
To garnish:
1 fresh red chilli, cut into rings
1 shallot, sliced
coriander leaves

- Serves 4–6
- Preparation time: about 15 minutes
- Cooking time: 15 minutes

Fast and Simple

Curries need not take hours to prepare:
cooks in Asian countries are just as busy
as cooks in the West! In recipes from
India and Sri Lanka, Thailand and
Malaysia, this chapter illustrates a wide
range of quick but authentic curries.
Some use very simple combinations of
spices, some are made with easily stored
homemade blends and others take
advantage of commercial curry powders
and pastes.

Thai Red Beef Curry

It is easy to produce an 'authentic' curry quickly, using either your own homemade Thai red curry paste, or one of the excellent ready-made versions now stocked by Asian shops and many supermarkets. It is illustrated on pages 30–31.

1 Heat the oil in a heavy-based saucepan and add the curry paste, ground coriander and cumin and the lime leaves. Cook over a gentle heat, stirring frequently, for 3 minutes.

2 Add the beef strips to the pan, mix to coat them evenly in the curry paste and cook gently, stirring frequently, for a further 5 minutes.

3 Add half the coconut milk to the pan, stir to combine and simmer gently for 4 minutes until most of the coconut milk has been absorbed.

4 Stir in the rest of the coconut milk with the peanut butter, fish sauce and sugar. Simmer gently for a further 5 minutes, until the sauce is thick and the beef is tender. Garnish with coriander sprigs, if using, and serve immediately with steamed rice.

3 tablespoons groundnut oil

3 tablespoons Thai red curry paste (see page 118)

½ teaspoon ground coriander

½ teaspoon ground cumin

4 Kaffir lime leaves, shredded

500 g/1 lb fillet of beef, cut into thin strips

400 ml/14 fl oz coconut milk

2 tablespoons crunchy peanut butter

2 teaspoons fish sauce

1 tablespoon soft brown sugar

sprigs of coriander, to garnish (optional)

- Serves 4
- Preparation time: 5–10 minutes
- Cooking time: about 20 minutes

Variation

Thai Green Chicken Curry

1 Cut 625 g/1¼ lb skinless, boneless chicken breasts or thighs into bite-sized pieces. Heat 3 tablespoons of groundnut oil in a heavy-based saucepan, add 4 tablespoons Thai green curry paste (see page 118), ½ teaspoon ground coriander, ½ teaspoon ground cumin and 5 Thai basil leaves, shredded. Cook over a gentle heat for 3 minutes.

2 Add the chicken, stir to coat evenly and cook gently for a further 5 minutes. Add 200 ml/7 fl oz coconut milk and simmer the curry for 4 minutes until most of the coconut milk has been absorbed.

3 Stir in another 200 ml/7 fl oz coconut milk, 2 teaspoons of fish sauce, 1 tablespoon soft brown sugar and 1 x 200 g/7 oz can of sliced bamboo shoots in water, drained. Mix well and simmer the curry for a further 6–8 minutes, until the chicken is cooked and the sauce is thick. Serve the curry hot, garnished with Thai basil leaves.

- Serves 4–6
- Preparation time: about 10 minutes
- Cooking time: 20 minutes

Prawn and Mango Curry

This quick and simple curry is illustrated on pages 30–31.

I Heat the oil in a heavy-based saucepan, add the onion and garlic and cook over a gentle heat, stirring frequently, for about 4 minutes or until softened. Stir in the curry paste and cook for a further 2 minutes.

2 Add the coconut milk and lime juice to the pan, stir to mix and simmer the curry sauce for 3 minutes. Add the ground almonds, prawns and some salt, to taste, and then simmer the curry gently for a further 3 minutes until all the prawns have turned pink and the curry sauce has thickened slightly.

3 Stir the diced mango into the curry and heat through for 1 minute. Taste and adjust the seasoning if necessary. Transfer the curry to a serving dish, scatter over the chopped coriander and serve immediately.

2 tablespoons groundnut oil

I red onion, finely chopped

2 garlic cloves, crushed

4 tablespoons mild curry paste

400 ml/14 fl oz coconut milk

juice of I lime

2 tablespoons ground almonds

24 uncooked peeled prawns

I small ripe mango, peeled and diced

2 tablespoons coarsely chopped fresh coriander

salt

- Serves 4
- Preparation time: 10 minutes
- Cooking time: 15 minutes

King Prawn and Coconut Curry

I Place all the ingredients for the spice paste in a blender or spice mill and blend to produce a thick paste. Heat the oil in a heavy-based saucepan, add the blended paste and turmeric and then cook over a gentle heat, stirring frequently, for just 3 minutes.

2 Add 150 ml/¼ pint water to the pan, mix well and simmer gently for 3 minutes. Stir in the coconut milk, lime juice, sugar and some salt to taste and simmer for a further 3 minutes.

3 Add the prawns to the curry and cook for 4–5 minutes until they have turned pink and are cooked through. Taste the curry and adjust the amount of salt if necessary.

4 Transfer the curry to a serving dish, garnish with the spring onions and toasted coconut and serve hot.

2 tablespoons groundnut oil

I teaspoon turmeric

150 ml/¼ pint coconut milk

juice of I lime

2 teaspoons soft brown sugar

16 uncooked peeled, king prawns

salt

Spice Paste:

2 fresh red chillies, deseeded and chopped

2 shallots, chopped

I stalk of lemon grass, chopped

2.5 cm/I inch piece of fresh root ginger, grated

¼ teaspoon shrimp paste

To garnish:

sliced spring onions

toasted flaked coconut

- Serves 4
- Preparation time: 10 minutes
- Cooking time: 15 minutes

33

Sweet Potato and Spinach Curry

Serve this curry at once with naan or chapati. This delicious recipe is illustrated opposite.

1 Cook the sweet potato chunks in a pan of salted boiling water for 8–10 minutes or until they are tender. Drain and set them aside.

2 Heat the oil in a saucepan, add the onion, garlic, shrimp paste and turmeric and then fry over a gentle heat, stirring frequently, for 3 minutes. Stir in the chilli and fry for a further 2 minutes.

3 Add the coconut milk, stir to mix and simmer for 3–4 minutes until the coconut milk has thickened slightly. Stir in the sweet potatoes and some salt, to taste, and cook the curry for 4 minutes.

4 Stir in the spinach, cover the pan and simmer gently for 2–3 minutes or until the spinach has wilted and the curry has heated through. Taste and adjust the seasoning if necessary and serve immediately.

500 g/1 lb sweet potato, peeled and cut into large chunks

3 tablespoons groundnut oil

1 red onion, chopped

2 garlic cloves, crushed

1 teaspoon shrimp paste

1 teaspoon turmeric

1 large fresh red chilli, deseeded and chopped

400 ml/14 fl oz coconut milk

250 g/8 oz ready-washed young leaf spinach

salt

- Serves 4
- Preparation time: about 10 minutes
- Cooking time: about 25 minutes

Malaysian Sardine Curry

This is a popular store-cupboard curry in Malaysia; it uses canned sardines, but for a different curry you could replace the sardines with canned salmon.

1 Heat the oil in a saucepan, add the onion, garlic and ginger and fry over a gentle heat, stirring frequently for about 4 minutes or until softened but not coloured. Add the mustard seeds and curry leaves and cook for a further 2 minutes.

2 Stir in the curry paste and cook, stirring, for 2 minutes, then add the coconut milk and salt, stir well and simmer the sauce for 5 minutes until it has thickened slightly.

3 Add the tomatoes, then cover the pan and cook the curry for a further 5 minutes. Break the sardines into large chunks and add them to the pan with the sauce from the can. Simmer the curry gently for a further 3 minutes. Taste and adjust the amount of salt if necessary, then serve garnished with the sliced green chillies and coriander leaves.

- Serves 4
- Preparation time: about 5 minutes
- Cooking time: 20–25 minutes

3 tablespoons vegetable oil

1 onion, sliced

2 garlic cloves, crushed

1 tablespoon grated fresh root ginger

1 teaspoon black mustard seeds

6 dried curry leaves

2 tablespoons curry paste for seafood

300 ml/½ pint coconut milk

½ teaspoon salt

3 small tomatoes, cut into wedges

1 x 475 g/15 oz can of sardines in tomato sauce

To garnish:

2 green chillies, sliced

2 tablespoons fresh coriander leaves

Variation

Sardine and Aubergine Curry

1 The ingredients are almost the same as in the main recipe, with the addition of 4 baby aubergines (weighing about 150g/5 oz in total), cut into wedges, and 1 extra tomato.

2 Follow step 1 of the main recipe. At Step 2, add the aubergines with the coconut milk and salt and simmer for 5 minutes until the sauce has thickened slightly.

3 Add 4 small tomatoes, cut into wedges the continue as in the main recipe.

- Serves 4–6
- Preparation time: about 10 minutes
- Cooking time: 25 minutes

Mixed Vegetable Curry

1 Heat the oil in a heavy-based saucepan, add the onion and fry over a gentle heat, stirring occasionally for about 4 minutes or until softened but not coloured. Stir in the cardamom pods, coriander, cumin, chilli powder and turmeric and fry for a further minute.

2 Add the carrots, aubergine, the stock and a good pinch of salt. Stir well, bring to the boil then reduce the heat and simmer, covered, for 10 minutes, stirring occasionally.

3 Stir in the courgettes, green beans and the yogurt. Cook the curry, uncovered, for 15 minutes, stirring occasionally.

4 Stir in the chopped coriander and cashew nuts. Heat through for 1 minute, then taste and adjust the seasoning if necessary. Transfer the curry to a warm serving dish. Drizzle over the yogurt, garnish with sprigs of coriander and serve hot.

3 tablespoons vegetable oil

1 onion, finely chopped

6 cardamom pods, bruised

2 teaspoons coriander seeds, lightly crushed

2 teaspoons cumin seeds, lightly crushed

1½ teaspoons chilli powder

1 teaspoon turmeric

175 g/6 oz carrots, sliced

175 g/6 oz aubergine, roughly chopped

300 ml/½ pint vegetable stock

175 g/6 oz courgettes, sliced

175 g/6 oz green beans, topped and tailed and cut into 2.5 cm/1 inch lengths

150 ml/¼ pint natural yogurt

2 tablespoons chopped fresh coriander

50 g/2 oz toasted cashew nuts, roughly chopped

salt

To garnish:

1 tablespoon natural yogurt

a few sprigs of coriander

- Serves 4–6
- Preparation time: about 10 minutes
- Cooking time: 30–35 minutes

Tamil Dry Potato Curry

1 Scrub the potatoes and cook them in a pan of salted boiling water for 25 minutes or until they are cooked. Drain and refresh them in cold water. When they are cool enough to handle, peel and cut them into 2.5 cm/1 inch chunks. Place the potato chunks in a bowl, add the chilli powder and season generously with salt. Toss to coat the potatoes evenly.

2 Heat the ghee in a large, heavy-based frying pan, add the onions and fry, stirring occasionally, for 5 minutes or until softened and lightly golden.

3 Stir in the chilli-coated potatoes and the curry leaves and fry over a very low heat, stirring, for 10 minutes or until the potatoes and onions are golden and the flavours are well combined. Taste and adjust the seasoning if necessary and serve the curry immediately.

500 g/1 lb waxy potatoes

1½ tablespoons chilli powder

3 tablespoons ghee

2 large onions, sliced thinly

6 curry leaves

salt

- Serves 4–6
- Preparation time: about 5 minutes
- Cooking time: 40–45 minutes

Simple Beef Curry with Spinach

If you would like to make this curry hotter, add some of the chilli seeds to it. This dish is illustrated opposite.

1 Heat the ghee or oil in a saucepan, add the onion and garlic and fry over a gentle heat, stirring frequently, for about 5 minutes or until softened but not coloured. Stir in the chillies and fry for a further 2 minutes.

2 Add the cloves, garam masala, coriander, turmeric, chilli powder and cumin. Stir well to mix and fry, stirring constantly, for 2 minutes.

3 Stir in the beef and salt and cook, stirring, for 3 minutes to seal the meat, then add the diced tomatoes, coconut milk and spinach and stir to mix. Cover the pan and then simmer the curry gently, stirring just occasionally, for 20 minutes.

4 Stir in the lemon juice and cook the curry, uncovered, for a further 8–10 minutes, stirring occasionally, until the sauce has thickened. Taste and adjust the seasoning if necessary and serve immediately. Saffron rice would be a good accompaniment to this curry.

2 tablespoons ghee or vegetable oil

1 large onion, thinly sliced

2 garlic cloves, crushed

2 green chillies, deseeded and sliced

2 whole cloves, bruised

1 teaspoon garam masala (see page 117)

1 teaspoon ground coriander

1 teaspoon turmeric

½ teaspoon chilli powder

1½ teaspoons ground cumin

625 g/1¼ lb fillet of beef, cut into bite-sized pieces

1 teaspoon salt

175 g/6 oz tomatoes, cut into large dice

150 ml/¼ pint coconut milk

250 g/8 oz ready-washed young leaf spinach

1 teaspoon lemon juice

- Serves 4
- Preparation time: about 20 minutes
- Cooking time: 35–40 minutes

Variation

Lamb and Spinach Curry

1 For this variation, you should use almost the same ingredients as in the main recipe, with lamb fillet replacing the fillet of beef, cut into bite-sized pieces.

2 Follow the cooking method described in the main recipe.

- Serves 4
- Preparation time: about 20 minutes
- Cooking time: 35–40 minutes

Chickpea Chole

A deliciously fragrant vegetarian curry, which goes very well with puris (see page 16). It is illustrated on page 39.

1 Heat the oil in a heavy-based saucepan, add the onion, garlic and ginger and fry over a gentle heat, stirring frequently, for about 5 minutes or until softened but not coloured.

2 Stir in the ground cumin, coriander, chilli powder and turmeric and fry for 2 minutes. Add the chickpeas, tomatoes, sugar and some salt to taste, and stir to combine the ingredients. Cover the pan and simmer the curry gently, stirring occasionally, for 10 minutes.

3 Stir in 1 tablespoon of the lime juice and the torn coriander leaves and heat through for a further 2 minutes. Taste the curry and add the remaining lime juice and more salt if necessary. Serve the chole hot, garnished with the coriander sprigs and slices of red onion.

3 tablespoons vegetable oil

1 onion, chopped

2 garlic cloves, crushed

2.5 cm/1 inch piece of fresh root ginger, grated

4 teaspoons ground cumin

1 tablespoon ground coriander

2 teaspoons chilli powder

1 teaspoon turmeric

2 x 425 g/14 oz cans of chickpeas, drained and rinsed

1 x 400 g/13 oz can of chopped tomatoes

1½ teaspoons soft brown sugar

1–2 tablespoons lime juice (depending on taste)

4 tablespoons torn fresh coriander leaves

salt

To garnish:

3 sprigs of coriander

½ red onion, sliced

- Serves 4–6
- Preparation time: 5–10 minutes
- Cooking time: 20 minutes

Variation

Chicken and Chickpea Chole

1 The ingredients and cooking method are almost the same as in the main recipe, but you will also need 300 g/10 oz skinless, boneless chicken thighs, cut into bite-sized pieces. Use only 1 x 425 g/14 oz can of chickpeas.

2 Follow step 1 of the main recipe. At step 2, after frying the spices for 2 minutes, add the chicken and fry, stirring occasionally, for a further 5 minutes.

3 Stir in the tomatoes, chickpeas, drained and rinsed, sugar and salt to taste, then continue as in the main recipe.

- Serves 4–6
- Preparation time: 5–10 minutes
- Cooking time: 25–30 minutes

Spicy Minced Beef and Pea Curry

1 Heat the oil in a heavy-based saucepan, add the chopped onion, garlic, ginger, garam masala and chilli powder and fry over a gentle heat, stirring frequently, for about 5 minutes or until softened.

2 Add the curry paste, tomato purée, beef and salt, and mix well so that all the ingredients are evenly coated in the spice mixture. Fry, stirring occasionally, for a further 5 minutes.

3 Stir in the peas and vegetable stock and then cover the pan. Simmer the curry gently for a further 5 minutes. Stir in the chopped coriander and taste and adjust the amount of salt if necessary. Transfer the curry to a warm serving dish, garnish with sprigs of fresh coriander and then serve immediately.

2 tablespoons vegetable oil

1 onion, chopped

2 garlic cloves, crushed

2.5 cm/1 inch piece of fresh root ginger, finely chopped

1 teaspoon garam masala (see page 117)

1 teaspoon chilli powder

3 tablespoons hot curry paste

1 tablespoon tomato purée

500 g/1 lb lean minced beef

1 teaspoon salt

175 g/6 oz frozen peas, defrosted

150 ml/¼ pint vegetable stock

3 tablespoons chopped fresh coriander

sprigs of coriander, to garnish

- Serves 4
- Preparation time: 5 minutes
- Cooking time: 20 minutes

Variation

Minced Lamb, Pea and Potato Curry

1 The ingredients and cooking method are as described in the main recipe, except that you substitute minced lamb for the minced beef, and use only 75 g/3 oz peas, adding 175 g/6 oz cooked, diced potato.

- Serves 4
- Preparation time: 5–10 minutes
- Cooking time: 20 minutes

41

Chicken Korma with Green Beans

This delicious recipe is illustrated opposite.

1 Heat the oil in a saucepan, add the chicken and onions, and fry over a gentle heat, stirring occasionally, for 6 minutes or until the onion is soft and the chicken is lightly coloured. Stir in the curry powder and cook for a further 2 minutes.

2 Add the stock, tomato purée, sugar, tomatoes, cream and a little salt. Stir to combine the ingredients, bring to the boil, then reduce the heat, cover the pan and simmer gently for 10 minutes, stirring occasionally.

3 Stir the beans into the curry and cook, covered, for a further 15–20 minutes, stirring occasionally, until the chicken is cooked and the beans are tender. Stir the ground almonds into the curry and simmer for 1 minute to thicken the sauce. Taste and adjust the seasoning if necessary. Serve the korma hot, garnished with toasted flaked almonds.

2 tablespoons vegetable oil

375 g/12 oz skinless, boneless chicken breasts, cut into bite-sized pieces

1 onion, sliced

2½ tablespoons korma curry powder

150 ml/¼ pint chicken stock

1 teaspoon tomato purée

2 teaspoons caster sugar

75 g/3 oz tomatoes, roughly chopped

150 ml/¼ pint single cream

125 g/4 oz green beans, topped and tailed and cut into 2.5 cm/1 inch lengths

25 g/1 oz ground almonds

salt

toasted flaked almonds, to garnish

- Serves 4
- Preparation time: 10–15 minutes
- Cooking time: 40 minutes

Okra Masala

Serve this dish immediately. It is illustrated opposite.

1 Heat the oil in a heavy-based saucepan, add the cumin, fennel, mustard and sesame seeds and fry over a gentle heat, stirring, for 1 minute. Stir in the onion and garlic and then fry, stirring occasionally, for a further 3 minutes.

2 Add 3 tablespoons of water, the sugar, tomato purée and curry paste, mix well and cook over a gentle heat for 1 minute.

3 Stir in the okra and season with salt. Add 200 ml/7 fl oz water to the pan and stir well. Bring the curry to the boil, then reduce the heat and simmer the curry gently for 10 minutes, stirring occasionally, until the okra are tender. Taste and adjust the seasoning if necessary. Serve hot.

3 tablespoons groundnut oil

1 teaspoon cumin seeds

½ teaspoon fennel seeds

½ teaspoon mustard seeds

1 teaspoon sesame seeds

1 onion, finely chopped

2 garlic cloves, crushed

1 tablespoon soft brown sugar

1 tablespoon tomato purée

2 tablespoons Madras curry paste (see page 117)

500 g/1 lb small okra, stalks trimmed

salt

- Serves 6
- Preparation time: about 5 minutes
- Cooking time: 15–20 minutes

Masoor Dhal

Use mustard oil, which is available from Indian supermarkets, instead of vegetable oil in this recipe to produce a sweeter, more fragrant dish.

1 Heat half the oil in a heavy-based saucepan, add the onion, garlic and ginger and fry over a gentle heat, stirring frequently, for about 5 minutes or until softened but not coloured. Add the turmeric, bay leaves and chillies and fry for 1 minute.

2 Add the drained lentils and stir to coat them evenly in the spices. Season generously and add 500 ml/17 fl oz water. Bring to the boil, then reduce the heat, cover the pan and simmer gently, stirring occasionally, for 15–20 minutes or until the lentils are cooked.

3 While the dhal is cooking, heat the remaining oil in a small frying pan, add the coconut, chilli powder, cumin, fennel and kalonji seeds and fry, stirring, for 2 minutes or until fragrant.

4 Stir the cooked spices into the dhal, with the sugar. Cook, stirring frequently, for a further 3 minutes. Taste and adjust the seasoning if necessary and serve hot, garnished with the toasted desiccated coconut.

- Serves 4
- Preparation time: 10 minutes
- Cooking time: about 30 minutes

3 tablespoons vegetable oil

I large onion, sliced

2 garlic cloves, crushed

2.5 cm/I inch piece of fresh root ginger, finely chopped

I teaspoon turmeric

2 bay leaves

2 small dried red chillies

250 g/8 oz red split lentils (masoor dhal), rinsed

2 tablespoons desiccated coconut

I teaspoon chilli powder

½ teaspoon cumin seeds

½ teaspoon fennel seeds

¼ teaspoon black onion seeds (kalonji)

I teaspoon sugar

salt and pepper

toasted desiccated coconut, to garnish

Variation

Spicy Moong Dhal

1 The ingredients and cooking method are almost the same as in the main recipe, but you should begin by soaking 250 g/8 oz moong dhal in cold water for 30 minutes.

2 Fry the onion and spices as in Step 1 of the main recipe, replacing the bay leaves with 3 curry leaves. Drain the beans, add them to the pan and season as in step 2. Add 400 ml/14 fl oz water, bring to the boil, then reduce the heat, cover the pan and simmer gently, stirring occasionally, for about 20 minutes or until the beans are cooked.

3 Fry the spices as in Step 3, replacing the fennel seeds with ½ teaspoon black mustard seeds.

4 Finish the recipe as in Step 4 and serve the dhal hot, garnished with sliced red chilli and chopped fresh coriander.

- Serves 4
- Preparation time: 10 minutes, plus 30 minutes soaking time
- Cooking time: about 30 minutes

Cauliflower Curry

1 Place the cumin, fennel, mustard and sesame seeds in a pestle and mortar and crush them lightly. Heat the oil in a heavy-based saucepan, add the crushed spices and fry them for 30 seconds. Add the onion and garlic and fry over a gentle heat, stirring, for 3 minutes.

2 Stir in 2 tablespoons water, the curry paste, tomato purée, sugar and tomatoes and cook over a gentle heat, stirring frequently, for 2 minutes. Add the cauliflower, green pepper, green chilli and salt, and stir to coat all the ingredients evenly in the spice mixture.

3 Add the coconut milk and 200 ml/7 fl oz water to the pan. Bring to the boil, then reduce the heat, cover the pan and simmer the curry gently for about 10 minutes or until the cauliflower is cooked, stirring from time to time. Taste and adjust the amount of salt if necessary. Serve the curry hot, with steamed rice.

- Serves 4
- Preparation time: 15 minutes
- Cooking time: 25 minutes

I teaspoon cumin seeds

½ teaspoon fennel seeds

½ teaspoon black mustard seeds

½ teaspoon sesame seeds

3 tablespoons vegetable oil

I onion, sliced

4 garlic cloves, chopped

2 tablespoons hot curry paste

I tablespoon tomato purée

2 teaspoons soft brown sugar

175 g/6 oz tomatoes, chopped roughly

500 g/I lb cauliflower, cut into small florets

I green pepper, deseeded and diced

I green chilli, deseeded and sliced thinly

½ teaspoon salt

150 ml/¼ pint coconut milk

Mild Egg Curry

Dhana jeera is a spice mixture made up of ground roasted coriander and cumin. A standard mix would be 2 parts coriander to 1 part cumin.

1 Heat the oil in a heavy-based saucepan, add the shallots, garlic, ginger, cinnamon stick and chilli, and fry over a gentle heat, stirring occasionally, for 3 minutes. Stir in the dhana jeera, curry leaves, saffron and its water and the salt, and fry for a further 2 minutes.

2 Add the coconut milk to the pan, stir to combine the ingredients, bring the curry sauce to the boil and boil for 4–5 minutes, until the sauce has thickened slightly. Reduce the heat, stir in the eggs and simmer the curry gently for 2 minutes. Taste and adjust the seasoning if necessary.

3 Transfer the curry to a warm serving dish. Scatter over the chopped coriander and bawang goreng, if using and serve the curry immediately.

- Serves 4
- Preparation time: about 25 minutes
- Cooking time: about 10 minutes

2 tablespoons vegetable oil

2 shallots, chopped

2 garlic cloves, crushed

2.5 cm/I inch piece of fresh root ginger, finely chopped

5 cm/2 inch piece of cinnamon stick, broken in half

I large fresh red chilli, deseeded and chopped

2 teaspoons dhana jeera

5 curry leaves

½ teaspoon saffron threads soaked in 2 tablespoons boiling water for 10 minutes

½ teaspoon salt

450 ml/¾ pint coconut milk

4 hard-boiled eggs, halved lengthways

To garnish:

2 tablespoons chopped fresh coriander

bawang goreng (see page 113)

45

Indian
subcontinent

From Kashmir and the snowy Himalaya mountains in the north to the warm seas, tropical forests and lush gardens of Kerala in the south, the very different climates of this vast subcontinent produce an enormous variety of ingredients. Historical influences, from Persian to Portuguese, also vary from region to region: there is no such thing as a typical Indian curry, but a kaleidoscope of tastes reflecting distant origins.

Kerala Prawn Curry

Southern Indian curries are traditionally fairly spicy as is this Kerala Prawn Curry – the spiciness coming from the number of dried chillies which are used in the recipe. It is illustrated on pages 46–47.

1 Place the ingredients for the spice mixture in an electric spice mill and grind to a fine powder, or grind with a pestle and mortar.

2 Heat the oil in a large, heavy-based saucepan, add the onion, garlic and ginger, and cook, stirring occasionally, for about 3 minutes until softened.

3 Stir in the ground spice mixture and cook, stirring constantly, for a further 2 minutes.

4 Add the tomatoes, coconut milk and salt, and simmer for 6–8 minutes to reduce the sauce and thicken it slightly.

5 Stir in the lime juice and sugar, then add the prawns and simmer the curry gently for about 8 minutes, until the prawns have turned pink. Transfer the curry to a serving dish and scatter over the spring onion. Serve the curry at once with steamed rice.

2 tablespoons groundnut oil

1 onion, finely chopped

3 garlic cloves, crushed

2.5 cm/1 inch piece of fresh root ginger, peeled and cut into julienne strips

125 g/4 oz tomatoes, roughly chopped

200 ml/7 fl oz coconut milk

½ teaspoon salt

juice of 1 lime

2 teaspoons caster sugar

20 large prawns, about 375 g/12 oz total weight

1 spring onion, sliced into julienne strips, to garnish

Spice Mixture:

3 tablespoons desiccated coconut, lightly toasted

6 small dried red chillies, roughly chopped

10 black peppercorns

1 teaspoon cumin seeds

1 teaspoon turmeric

- Serves 4
- Preparation time: 10–15 minutes
- Cooking time: about 25 minutes

Steamed Tuna Fish Curry in Banana Leaves

This is a very fresh-tasting curry, illustrated on pages 46–47. If banana leaves are unavailable, wrap the tuna steaks in a double thickness of buttered greaseproof paper for steaming.

1 Place the tuna steaks in a shallow, non-metallic dish and pour over the lime juice. Cover and set aside to marinate while preparing the curry paste.

2 Place the cumin and coriander seeds in a blender and process briefly. Add the chillies, mint, ginger and garlic, and blend for 1 minute to produce a paste. Add the sugar, salt, coconut and vinegar, and blend again until all the ingredients are thoroughly combined.

3 Lay the pieces of banana leaf (or buttered greaseproof paper) on a flat surface. Remove the tuna from the lime juice and place a steak in the centre of each banana leaf. Spread the green curry paste over the tuna, completely covering the fish. Wrap up the banana leaves to enclose the fish, and secure with cocktail sticks.

4 Steam the fish over boiling water for 18–20 minutes or until the fish flakes when tested with the point of a knife.

5 Garnish the steamed curry with onion and chilli rings and mint sprigs, and serve with wedges of lime.

4 x 150 g/5 oz fresh tuna steaks

juice of 1 lime

4 large pieces of banana leaf

Green Curry Paste:

1 tablespoon cumin seeds

2 tablespoons coriander seeds

3 large green chillies, deseeded and chopped

25 g/1 oz fresh mint leaves

5 cm/2 inch piece of fresh root ginger, grated

4 garlic cloves, crushed

25 g/1 oz caster sugar

½ teaspoon salt

75 g/3 oz desiccated coconut

50 ml/2 fl oz malt vinegar

To garnish:

1 onion, cut into rings

2 green chillies, deseeded and cut into rings

sprigs of mint

lime wedges

- Serves 4
- Preparation time: about 10 minutes
- Cooking time: 20 minutes

Fish Molee

This mild curry, cooked in rich coconut milk, comes from southern India. A similar curry is made in Sri Lanka, where it is called 'White Curry'.

1 Rub the fish fillets with the turmeric and salt and set them aside while you prepare the curry sauce.

2 Heat the ghee or oil in a heavy-based saucepan, add the onion, garlic and ginger, and fry over a gentle heat for about 3 minutes, until softened.

3 Stir in the curry powder and chillies and cook, stirring constantly, for a further 2 minutes.

4 Add the coconut milk and bring to the boil, stirring constantly, then reduce the heat and simmer the curry gravy for about 5 minutes or until it has thickened slightly.

5 Add the fish and cook gently for a further 6–8 minutes or until the fish flakes when tested with the point of a knife. Taste and adjust the seasoning if necessary. Serve hot.

4 x 150 g/5 oz cod or haddock fillets

½ teaspoon turmeric

1 teaspoon salt

2 tablespoons ghee or vegetable oil

1 onion, chopped finely

3 garlic cloves, crushed

1 tablespoon freshly grated root ginger

1 tablespoon basic Indian curry powder (see page 116)

2 fresh red chillies, quartered lengthways and deseeded

450 ml/¾ pint thick coconut milk

- Serves 4
- Preparation time: about 10 minutes
- Cooking time: 20 minutes

Variation

Cochin Prawn Curry

A classic dish from the Malabar coast, in which the addition of tamarind adds tang to a coconut milk-based curry.

1 Rub 20 uncooked peeled, prawns (approximate weight 300 g/10 oz) with ½ teaspoon turmeric and 1 teaspoon salt. Set aside while preparing the curry.

2 Heat 2 tablespoons of ghee or vegetable oil in a pan and fry 1 onion, finely chopped, 3 garlic cloves, crushed, and 1 tablespoon of grated fresh root ginger over a gentle heat for 3 minutes, until softened.

3 Stir in 4 tablespoons chopped fresh coriander, 1 tablespoon basic Indian curry powder (see page 116) and 2 fresh green chillies, quartered lengthways and deseeded. Cook for 2 minutes.

4 Dissolve 1 tablespoon tamarind pulp in 150 ml/¼ pint boiling water, then press it through a sieve into the pan with the fried ingredients. Stir in 150 ml/¼ pint thick coconut milk. Bring the curry gravy to the boil, stirring constantly, then reduce the heat and simmer for 5 minutes or until it has thickened slightly.

5 Stir in the prawns and cook gently for 5 minutes or until they have turned pink and are cooked through. Taste and adjust the seasoning and serve at once.

- Serves 4
- Preparation time: about 15 minutes
- Cooking time: 15–20 minutes

49

Lamb Dhansak

Dhansak is a Parsee dish from western India. It is traditionally served on special occasions. It is very nutritious, containing lentils and vegetables. It is illustrated opposite.

I Wash the lentils, chickpeas and moong dhal and soak them overnight in cold water.

2 The next day, drain the lentils and place them in a large saucepan with the cubed lamb. Pour over enough boiling water to cover the lentils and meat and season generously with salt. Bring to the boil, skim any scum from the surface, then cover and simmer the lentils and meat, stirring occasionally, for about 20 minutes.

3 Add all the prepared vegetables to the pan, stir well and continue cooking for a further 40 minutes, until the lentils and vegetables are cooked and the lamb is tender. Drain the liquid from the pan and remove the pieces of meat using a slotted spoon. Set the meat aside and tip the cooked vegetables and lentils into a blender or food processor. Blend to produce a thick purée.

4 Heat the ghee in a large, heavy-based sauté pan and fry the onion over a gentle heat for 5 minutes, until it is softened and golden.

5 Place all the ingredients for the masala mixture in a food processor and blend to a paste. Add this paste to the softened onion and cook over a low heat for a further 3 minutes. Stir in the dry spice mixture and cook, stirring constantly, for 3 minutes, until the mixture is aromatic.

50 g/2 oz red lentils

50 g/2 oz chickpeas

50 g/2 oz moong dhal

750 g/1½ lb lamb fillet cut into 5 cm/2 inch cubes

3 tablespoons ghee

I large onion, thinly sliced

2 tablespoons tomato purée

salt and pepper

deep-fried onion slices, to garnish

Vegetables:

300 g/10 oz aubergine, cubed

250 g/8 oz pumpkin, peeled and cubed

125 g/4 oz potato, peeled and cubed

2 onions, chopped roughly

2 tomatoes, skinned and chopped

75 g/3 oz fresh spinach, washed

Masala Mixture:

3 fresh red chillies, deseeded and chopped

3 green chillies, deseeded and chopped

6 garlic cloves, crushed

2.5 cm/1 inch piece of fresh root ginger, finely chopped

25 g/1 oz fresh coriander leaves

15 g/½ oz fresh mint leaves

4 tablespoons water

Dry Spice Mixture:

2 teaspoons turmeric

I teaspoon black mustard seeds

½ teaspoon ground cinnamon

¼ teaspoon fenugreek powder

2 tablespoons dhana jeera powder

4 cardamom pods, crushed

6 Add the lamb and the lentil vegetable purée to the pan, together with the tomato purée and 300 ml/½ pint water. Season generously, cover and simmer the curry for about 30 minutes until it is thick. If it becomes too dry during cooking, add a little more water to the pan. Taste and adjust the seasoning if necessary.

7 Transfer the dhansak to a serving dish, garnish with deep-fried onions and serve at once with plain or saffron rice.

- Serves 6
- Preparation time: about 30 minutes, plus overnight soaking time
- Cooking time: 1¾ hours

Duck Vindaloo

This is a traditional hot and sour curry which originates from the former Portuguese colony of Goa. The vinegar in the recipe acts as a pickling agent, enabling this curry to be made a few days in advance, if you wish.

1 Slice the duck breasts diagonally into 2.5 cm/1 inch thick slices and place them in a shallow non-metallic dish.

2 Place the chillies, vinegar, garlic, ginger, mustard seeds and peppercorns in a blender or food processor and blend to a smooth paste. Stir the ground coriander, cumin and turmeric into the paste.

3 Pour this spice mixture over the duck slices and mix until they are evenly coated. Cover and leave to marinate for 3 hours at room temperature or overnight in the refrigerator.

4 Heat the oil in a heavy-based saucepan. Remove the duck from the marinade, reserving the marinade, and add the duck to the pan with the salt. Cook over a gentle heat for 5 minutes, then pour away any excess fat from the pan. Add the reserved marinade together with 150 ml/¼ pint water and stir well. Cover and simmer, stirring, for 30 minutes, or until the duck is tender.

5 Stir in the sugar, increase the heat and cook the curry over a medium-high heat for 6–8 minutes, stirring frequently to prevent the curry sticking. The sauce should be of a thick, coating consistency. Serve hot, with basmati rice.

- Serves 4
- Preparation time: about 15 minutes, plus marinating time
- Cooking time: 45 minutes

750 g/1½ lb boneless duck breasts

6 medium dried red chillies, deseeded and chopped

150 ml/¼ pint distilled malt vinegar

6 garlic cloves, chopped

2.5 cm/1 inch piece of fresh root ginger, grated

1 teaspoon mustard seeds, lightly crushed

20 black peppercorns, lightly crushed

1 tablespoon ground coriander

1 tablespoon ground cumin

1 teaspoon turmeric

1 tablespoon vegetable oil

1 teaspoon salt

1 tablespoon soft brown sugar

Variation

Prawn Vindaloo

1 Blend together 6 medium dried red chillies, deseeded and chopped, 150 ml/¼ pint distilled malt vinegar, 6 garlic cloves, chopped, 2.5 cm/1 inch piece of fresh root ginger, grated, 1 teaspoon mustard seeds, lightly crushed, and 20 black peppercorns, lightly crushed.

2 Transfer the blended spice mixture to a bowl and stir in 1 tablespoon ground coriander, 1 tablespoon ground cumin and 1 teaspoon turmeric.

3 Heat 2 tablespoons of vegetable oil in a heavy-based saucepan, stir in the spice mixture and cook over a gentle heat, stirring constantly, for 5 minutes. Add 300 ml/½ pint water to the pan, stir well, then cover and simmer the sauce gently for 15 minutes.

4 Remove the lid from the pan, increase the heat and cook the sauce over a moderate heat for 5 minutes to reduce it to a thick, coating consistency.

5 Stir 1 teaspoon salt, 1 tablespoon soft brown sugar and 500 g/1 lb cooked peeled prawns into the sauce. Cook for 3 minutes or until the prawns are heated through. Serve at once with steamed or boiled rice.

- Serves 4
- Preparation time: about 5 minutes
- Cooking time: 30 minutes

Madras Fish Curry

A hot curry with the added tartness of tamarind – a favourite ingredient in Indian fish curries.

1 Rub the cod fillet with the turmeric and salt, and place in a shallow, non-metallic dish.
2 Soak the tamarind pulp in 300 ml/½ pint boiling water for 10 minutes, then strain the pulp through a sieve, pressing it against the sieve to extract as much tamarind flavour as possible. Discard the pulp and pour the tamarind liquid over the fish. Cover and marinate for 1 hour in the refrigerator.
3 Meanwhile, prepare the curry gravy. Heat the oil in a heavy-based sauté pan, add the curry leaves and kalonji seeds and cook gently for 1 minute.
4 Stir in the sliced onions and chillies and then cook for a further 3 minutes, until softened but not coloured. Stir in the curry paste and cook for a further 2 minutes.
5 Remove the fish from the tamarind liquid and set aside. Add the tamarind liquid to the pan of fried ingredients, with the tomatoes. Stir gently to mix, then simmer the curry gravy gently for 10 minutes.
6 Add the fish and coriander to the pan, cover and cook for a further 8 minutes or until the fish is just cooked through. Taste and adjust the seasoning if necessary and serve the curry hot, with steamed rice or rotis.

750 g/1½ lb skinless cod fillet, cut into 10 cm/4 inch pieces
1 teaspoon turmeric
½ teaspoon salt
1 tablespoon tamarind pulp
4 tablespoons groundnut oil
8 curry leaves
2 teaspoons onion seeds (kalonji)
2 onions, thinly sliced
2 large green chillies, deseeded and thinly sliced
2 tablespoons Madras curry paste (see page 117)
4 small tomatoes, quartered
4 tablespoons chopped fresh coriander

- Serves 4
- Preparation time: about 15 minutes, plus marinating time
- Cooking time: 25 minutes

Chicken Bhuna

Serve this dry chicken curry with Indian flat breads, such as chapatis or parathas.

1 Heat the ghee in a heavy-based saucepan, crumble the curry leaves and add them to the pan with the mustard seeds. Fry them over a gentle heat for 1 minute.
2 Place the onion, garlic and ginger in a blender or food processor and blend to a coarse paste. Add this paste to the fried curry leaves and mustard seeds and cook gently for a further 5 minutes.
3 Add the curry powder, garam masala, cumin, coriander and chilli powder, and cook, stirring constantly, for 2 minutes.
4 Add the chicken, salt and 150 ml/¼ pint water. Stir to coat the chicken evenly in the spice mixture, then cover the pan and cook the curry over a gentle heat, stirring occasionally, for about 20 minutes or until the chicken is tender.
5 Remove the lid, increase the heat and cook the curry for a further 3–5 minutes until thick and dry. Taste and adjust the seasoning if necessary and serve the curry at once.

3 tablespoons ghee
8 dried curry leaves
1 teaspoon black mustard seeds
1 large onion, chopped
4 garlic cloves, chopped
2.5 cm/1 inch piece of fresh root ginger, chopped
1 tablespoon basic Indian curry powder (see page 116)
1 teaspoon garam masala (see page 117)
1 teaspoon ground cumin
1 teaspoon ground coriander
2 teaspoons chilli powder
750 g/1½ lb skinless, boneless chicken breasts or thighs, cut into 2.5 cm/1 inch cubes
1 teaspoon salt

- Serves 4–6
- Preparation time: about 10 minutes
- Cooking time: 30 minutes

Chicken Makhani

Tomatoes and butter are the characteristic ingredients of a makhani, a refined and elegant dish.

1 Start by making the marinade. Place the chillies, garlic and cumin seeds in a blender or food processor and blend briefly before adding the remaining ingredients and blending to produce a paste.

2 Transfer the marinade to a non-metallic bowl. Add the chicken pieces to the marinade, turning to coat them evenly. Cover and refrigerate for 3 hours.

3 Meanwhile, prepare the sauce. Place the tomatoes in a large saucepan and cook them gently, with no added water, for about 20 minutes or until they are tender. Then rub them through a fine sieve into a clean saucepan. Simmer the tomato pulp, stirring occasionally, for about 50 minutes until it is thick and reduced.

4 Stir in the butter and some salt and cook the sauce over a medium heat, stirring often, for a further 30 minutes until it is thick. Stir in the cream and heat it through. Taste and adjust the amount of salt if necessary and set the sauce aside.

5 Heat the oil in a large, heavy-based sauté pan. Remove the chicken pieces from their marinade, reserving the marinade, and fry them gently to seal them, for about 5 minutes. Add the marinade to the pan, increase the heat and cook, stirring frequently, for a further 12 minutes or until the chicken is cooked through.

6 Reduce the heat and pour the tomato sauce over the chicken. Simmer gently for a further 5 minutes.

7 Transfer the chicken to a serving dish and garnish with a swirl of cream and a few coriander sprigs. Naan bread is a good accompaniment.

750 g/1½ lb skinless, boneless chicken breasts or thighs, cut into 5 cm/2 inch pieces

3 tablespoons vegetable oil

Marinade:

3 large red chillies, deseeded and chopped

4 garlic cloves, crushed

2 teaspoons toasted cumin seeds, crushed

1 teaspoon garam masala (see page 117)

½ teaspoon salt

2 tablespoons fresh coriander leaves

juice of 1 lemon

150 ml/¼ pint natural yogurt

Sauce:

1.5 kg/3 lb ripe tomatoes, quartered

50 g/2 oz butter

150 ml/¼ pint double cream

salt

To garnish:

1 tablespoon double cream

a few coriander sprigs

- Serves 6
- Preparation time: about 15 minutes, plus 3 hours marinating time
- Cooking time: 2¼ hours

54

Bangalore Chicken Curry

This 'green' curry from central southern India is made with a lot of fresh coriander and fresh green chillies.

1 Heat the ghee in a large, heavy-based sauté pan. Add the onions and fry over a medium heat, stirring frequently, for about 5 minutes or until they are softened and golden.

2 Stir in the garlic, turmeric and dhana jeera and cook, stirring, for a further 3 minutes.

3 Place the coriander leaves and green chillies in a blender or food processor and blend to a paste. Add this paste to the pan, reduce the heat to very low and cook, stirring constantly, for a further 10 minutes.

4 Add the chicken pieces to the pan, turn them in the spice mixture to coat them evenly, then add the stock, coconut milk and salt. Bring to the boil, then reduce the heat, cover and simmer, stirring and turning the chicken occasionally, for about 50 minutes or until the juices from the chicken run clear when tested with a skewer. Stir in the lemon juice and taste and adjust the amount of salt if necessary.

5 Transfer the cooked chicken pieces to a serving dish and keep them warm. Increase the heat and boil the curry sauce for 5–8 minutes to thicken it. Pour it over the chicken, garnish with coriander and serve at once.

3 tablespoons ghee

2 onions, thinly sliced

6 garlic cloves, chopped

1 teaspoon turmeric

1½ teaspoons ground dhana jeera

40 g/1½ oz fresh coriander leaves

3 large green chillies, deseeded and chopped

1 x 1.75 kg/3½ lb chicken jointed into 8 pieces

150 ml/¼ pint chicken stock

300 ml/½ pint coconut milk

1 teaspoon salt

1 tablespoon lemon juice

coriander leaves, to garnish

- Serves 6
- Preparation time: about 20 minutes
- Cooking time: 1 hour 20 minutes

Lamb Korma

A favourite rich, mild lamb curry cooked with yogurt, coconut, saffron and almonds.

1 Place the lamb in a bowl. Mix together the yogurt, saffron and its water and the salt. Pour over the lamb, cover and leave to marinate for 2 hours.

2 Place the ingredients for the blended mixture in a food processor and blend to produce a thick paste. Set aside.

3 Heat the ghee in a saucepan, add the cardamom, cinnamon, cumin and coriander, and cook over a gentle heat for 1 minute. Stir in the blended mixture and cook, stirring frequently, for a further 5 minutes.

4 Add the coconut milk, lamb and saffron yogurt, bring to the boil, then lower the heat, cover the pan and cook very gently, stirring occasionally, for 45 minutes or until the lamb is tender and the sauce is thick.

5 Stir in the chopped coriander and sugar and serve hot, garnished with coriander leaves and flaked almonds.

750 g/1½ lb boneless leg of lamb, cubed

150 ml/¼ pint natural yogurt

½ teaspoon saffron threads infused in 2 tablespoons boiling water for 10 minutes

1 teaspoon salt

2 tablespoons ghee

¼ teaspoon ground cardamom

½ teaspoon ground cinnamon

1½ teaspoons ground cumin

1½ teaspoons ground coriander

300 ml/½ pint coconut milk

2 tablespoons chopped fresh coriander

½ teaspoon caster sugar

Blended Mixture:

2 onions, chopped

3 garlic cloves, chopped

2.5 cm/1 inch piece of fresh root ginger, chopped

2 green chillies, deseeded and chopped

50 g/2 oz ground almonds

150 ml/¼ pint water

To garnish:

fresh coriander leaves

25 g/1 oz toasted flaked almonds

- Serves 4–6
- Preparation time: about 20 minutes, plus 2 hours marinating time
- Cooking time: about 1 hour

Lamb Doh Piaza

Doh means two and Piaza means onions, and onions are used in two ways in this recipe. Firstly, finely chopped in the spice mixture and then sliced, fried and added towards the end of the cooking time.

1 Melt 2 tablespoons of the ghee in a wide, heavy-based saucepan. Add 2 tablespoons of the oil and stir in the sliced onions. Fry the onions over a medium heat, stirring frequently, for about 10 minutes or until they are browned all over. Remove the onions from the pan and set aside.

2 Add the remaining ghee and 1 more tablespoon of oil to the pan and fry the lamb in batches until browned. Remove the lamb and set aside.

3 Add the remaining oil and all the ingredients for the spice mixture to the saucepan. Cook, stirring, for 1 minute then stir in the yogurt and then cook for a further minute.

4 Return the lamb to the pan. Stir well, cover and cook over a low heat, stirring occasionally, for 30 minutes until the meat is tender. (If the sauce appears to be drying out add a little water.)

5 Stir the reserved onions into the curry. Cover the pan and cook gently for a further 10 minutes. Taste and add more salt if necessary. Serve hot, garnished with coriander.

- Serves 4–6
- Preparation time: 30 minutes
- Cooking time: about 1 hour

3 tablespoons ghee

4 tablespoons vegetable oil

500 g/1 lb onions, sliced thinly

750 g/1½ lb lean lamb e.g. boneless leg or shoulder, cut into bite-sized pieces

150 ml/¼ pint natural yogurt

Spice Mixture:

1 large onion, chopped finely

4 garlic cloves, crushed

2 teaspoons freshly grated root ginger

1 teaspoon turmeric

1 teaspoon garam masala (see page 117)

2 teaspoons chilli powder

1 tablespoon ground coriander

1 tablespoon ground cumin

1 teaspoon salt

6 cardamom pods, bruised

2 tablespoons chopped fresh coriander, to garnish

Kashmir Kofta Curry

A fragrant meatball curry that would go well with Indian bread such Naan or Kulcha (see page 100).

1 To make the lamb meatballs, place the lamb, ginger, red chilli, coriander, 1 teaspoon of the garam masala, 1 teaspoon of the salt and the pepper in a bowl. Mix thoroughly then divide the mixture into 16 portions and shape each portion into a small meatball.

2 Heat the oil in a heavy-based frying pan, add the meatballs and fry over a gentle heat for 5 minutes, turning occasionally to seal them. Using a slotted spoon, transfer the meatballs to a saucepan.

3 Mix together the yogurt, sugar, chilli powder, the remaining garam masala and salt and 300 ml/½ pint water. Pour the yogurt mixture over the meatballs and then cook the curry, uncovered, over a medium heat for 10 minutes or until the meatballs are cooked and most of the liquid has been absorbed, leaving just a little sauce.

4 Serve the kofta curry hot, garnished with a good pinch of ground cardamom and coriander sprigs.

- Serves 4
- Preparation time: 30 minutes
- Cooking time: 20 minutes

500 g/1 lb lean minced lamb

1 tablespoon grated fresh root ginger

1 large red chilli, deseeded and very finely chopped

2 tablespoons chopped fresh coriander

1 tablespoon garam masala (see page 117)

1½ teaspoons salt

¼ teaspoon ground black pepper

3 tablespoons vegetable oil

150 ml/¼ pint natural yogurt

1 teaspoon soft brown sugar

½ teaspoon chilli powder

To garnish:

a generous pinch of ground cardamom

sprigs of fresh coriander

Cauliflower Pachadi

This is a traditional dish from Kerala in southern India, in which cauliflower is marinated in buttermilk before cooking. It is illustrated opposite.

1 Place the cauliflower florets in a bowl with the buttermilk, salt and some pepper. Mix well to combine the ingredients and set aside for 2 hours to allow the cauliflower to marinate in the buttermilk.

2 Heat the ghee in a heavy-based saucepan, add the onion, garlic and ginger, and fry over a gentle heat, stirring occasionally, for about 8 minutes, until softened and lightly golden.

3 Add the 2 types of mustard seeds, the turmeric and coconut, and cook for a further 3 minutes, stirring constantly.

4 Stir in the cauliflower with its buttermilk marinade and 150 ml/¼ pint water. Bring the curry to the boil, then reduce the heat, cover the pan and simmer gently for 12 minutes or until the cauliflower is tender.

5 Remove the lid, taste and adjust the seasoning if necessary and stir in the chopped coriander. Increase the heat and cook the cauliflower pachadi for a further 3–4 minutes to thicken the sauce. Serve hot as a vegetable accompaniment to other curries, with steamed rice or naan bread.

- Serves 4
- Preparation time: about 10 minutes, plus 2 hours marinating time
- Cooking time: about 30 minutes

375 g/12 oz cauliflower florets

150 ml/¼ pint buttermilk

1 teaspoon salt

3 tablespoons ghee

1 large onion, thinly sliced

2 garlic cloves, crushed

1 tablespoon freshly grated root ginger

1 teaspoon mustard seeds

1 teaspoon black mustard seeds

1 teaspoon turmeric

25 g/1 oz desiccated coconut

2 tablespoons chopped fresh coriander

freshly ground black pepper

Spinach Paneer

Paneer is Indian curd cheese and it is available from good Indian grocers. This dish is illustrated opposite.

1 Cut the paneer into 2.5 cm/1 inch cubes and set it aside. Steam the spinach for 3–4 minutes until it has wilted, leave it to cool and then place it in a food processor and blend briefly to purée it. Set it aside.

2 Heat the ghee in a heavy-based saucepan, add the paneer cubes and fry them, turning them occasionally, for 10 minutes or until they are golden all over. Remove them from the pan and set aside.

3 Add the onion, garlic, chilli and ginger to the hot ghee and fry gently over a low heat, stirring constantly, for 5 minutes, until softened. Stir in the turmeric, coriander, chilli powder and cumin, and fry for a further minute.

4 Add the puréed spinach and salt, stir well to combine, cover the pan and simmer gently for 5 minutes.

5 Stir in the fried paneer and cook, covered, for a further 5 minutes. Taste and adjust the seasoning if necessary, and serve immediately.

- Serves 4
- Preparation time: 15 minutes
- Cooking time: 30 minutes

250 g/8 oz paneer

375 g/12 oz young leaf spinach, washed and dried

2 tablespoons ghee

1 large onion, chopped

2 garlic cloves, crushed

1 large green chilli, deseeded and sliced

1 tablespoon grated fresh root ginger

1 teaspoon turmeric

1 teaspoon ground coriander

1 teaspoon chilli powder

½ teaspoon ground cumin

½ teaspoon salt

Mushroom Curry

1 Heat the ghee or oil in a heavy-based saucepan. Add the garlic, ginger and spring onions, and fry over a gentle heat, stirring occasionally, for 2 minutes or until softened.

2 Stir in the curry powder and mustard seeds and cook for a further 1 minute. Add the prepared mushrooms and the salt, stir to mix well and then cook, covered, for a further 5 minutes, stirring occasionally.

3 Add the garam masala and coconut milk and cook the curry uncovered for a further 4–5 minutes until the sauce has thickened slightly.

4 Stir in the lemon juice, taste and adjust the seasoning if necessary, garnish with chopped coriander and serve at once.

2 tablespoons ghee or vegetable oil

3 garlic cloves, crushed

1 teaspoon freshly grated root ginger

6 spring onions, sliced

1 tablespoon basic Indian curry powder (see page 116)

½ teaspoon mustard seeds

300 g/10 oz button mushrooms, halved

300 g/10 oz flat mushrooms, thickly sliced

1 teaspoon salt

1 teaspoon garam masala (see page 117)

150 ml/¼ pint thick coconut milk

juice of ½ lemon

1 tablespoon chopped fresh coriander, to garnish

- Serves 4
- Preparation time: about 10 minutes
- Cooking time: 15 minutes

Variation

Mushroom Curry with Peas and Potato

1 Follow step 1 of the main recipe.

2 Stir in 1 tablespoon basic Indian curry powder (see page 116) and ½ teaspoon black mustard seeds. Cook for about 1 minute, then add 250 g/8 oz flat mushrooms, thickly sliced, 375 g/12 oz peeled and cooked potato, cubed, and 1 teaspoon of salt. Stir to combine, then cover and cook gently for a further 5 minutes, stirring occasionally.

3 Add 1 teaspoon garam masala (see page 117), 150 ml/¼ pint thick coconut milk and 125 g/4 oz green peas. Cook the curry uncovered for a further 4–5 minutes.

4 Stir in the juice of ½ lemon, taste and adjust the seasoning if necessary and serve at once garnished with fresh coriander.

- Serves 4
- Preparation time: about 10 minutes
- Cooking time: 15 minutes

Goanese Lamb and Pork Curry

An unusual curry from Goa in which two types of meat are cooked together.

1 Heat the oil in a heavy-based saucepan, add the onions, garlic, ginger and chillies, and cook over a low heat, stirring frequently, for about 5 minutes until softened.

2 Place the ingredients for the spice mixture in a blender or spice mill and grind to produce a fine powder. Add the ground spices to the saucepan and fry for a further 1 minute.

3 Add the lamb pieces and pork, together with the salt. Coat the meat in the spices and cook for 2 minutes. Add 150 ml/¼ pint water and the vinegar to the pan and mix to combine the ingredients. Cover and simmer over a gentle heat, stirring occasionally, for about 45 minutes or until the meat is tender.

4 Remove the lid, increase the heat and cook for a further 15 minutes, stirring frequently, until the sauce is thick and dark. Taste and adjust the seasoning if necessary.

5 Transfer the curry to a serving dish and garnish with chilli rings. Serve with steamed white or saffron rice.

3 tablespoons vegetable oil
2 onions, finely chopped
3 garlic cloves, crushed
1 tablespoon grated fresh root ginger
2 large red chillies, quartered lengthways and deseeded
375 g/12 oz lamb fillet, cut into bite-sized pieces
375 g/12 oz lean pork, cut into bite-sized pieces
1 teaspoon salt
75 ml/3 fl oz distilled malt vinegar
Spice Mixture:
1 teaspoon ground cumin
1 teaspoon ground coriander
1 teaspoon chilli powder
1 tablespoon black mustard seeds
1 tablespoon black onion seeds (kalonji)
1 tablespoon garam masala (see page 117)
2 fresh green chillies, deseeded and cut into rings, to garnish

- Serves 6
- Preparation time: about 15 minutes
- Cooking time: 1¼ hours

Chicken and Yogurt Curry with Mint

1 Place the onion, garlic, mint leaves and ginger in a blender or food processor and blend to a smooth paste.

2 Heat the ghee in a large, heavy-based saucepan, add the blended paste and fry gently for 5 minutes.

3 Add the infused saffron with its water, the garam masala and chilli powder and fry for a further 1 minute.

4 Cut each chicken breast into 3 pieces and add them to the pan with the salt. Stir to coat the chicken in the spice mixture and cook for a further 5 minutes, to seal the chicken.

5 Add the yogurt and tomatoes, stir well, cover the pan and simmer gently for 15 minutes until the chicken is cooked.

6 Remove the lid and simmer uncovered for 4–5 minutes more to thicken the sauce slightly. Taste the sauce and adjust the amount of salt, if necessary.

7 Transfer the curry to a serving dish, garnish with mint sprigs and serve with boiled or steamed rice.

1 onion, chopped
4 garlic cloves, crushed
15 g/½ oz fresh mint leaves
1 tablespoon grated fresh root ginger
3 tablespoons ghee
½ teaspoon saffron threads, infused in 2 tablespoons of boiling water for 10 minutes
2 teaspoons garam masala (see page 117)
1 teaspoon chilli powder
750 g/1½ lb skinless, boneless chicken breasts
½ teaspoon salt
100 ml/3½ fl oz natural yogurt
175 g/6 oz tomatoes, chopped
sprigs of mint, to garnish

- Serves 4–6
- Preparation time: 15–20 minutes
- Cooking time: 35 minutes

Sri Lanka

Less than 30 miles separate Sri Lanka from the Indian state of Tamil Nadu, so it is not surprising that Sri Lankan curries share many of the features of southern Indian cooking, using ingredients such as fish and shellfish, and similar vegetables. An important difference lies in the basic curry powder, in which the spices are first toasted until they are quite dark, giving the curries a distinctive, full, roasted flavour.

Ceylon Crab Omelette Curry

Omelette curry is a Sri Lankan speciality and the addition of crab makes it really delicious. Do try to use fresh crab meat if possible although canned crab meat may be used instead. This dish is illustrated on pages 62–63.

1 To prepare the omelette, place the beaten eggs in a large bowl and add the crab meat, shallots, chilli, coriander and lemon juice. Season the mixture generously with salt and pepper and mix everything together until well combined.

2 Heat the oil in a heavy-based frying pan and pour in the omelette mixture. Cook the omelette over a medium heat for 5 minutes or until it is firm underneath then place the omelette pan under a preheated grill and cook the omelette for a further 5 minutes or until it is cooked through. Remove the cooked omelette from the pan, roll it up and set it aside while preparing the curry sauce.

3 Place the shallots, chillies, coconut and fennel seeds in a blender or food processor and blend briefly to produce a paste. Heat the oil in a large heavy-based saucepan, add the ground coriander, cumin and the chilli powder, and then fry the mixture over a gentle heat for a few seconds or until fragrant. Add the shallots and chilli paste to the pan and fry gently, stirring occasionally, for about 5 minutes.

4 eggs, beaten

150 g/5 oz flaked crab meat

2 shallots, finely chopped

1 large fresh red chilli, deseeded and finely chopped

1 tablespoon chopped fresh coriander

1 teaspoon lemon juice

1 tablespoon vegetable oil

salt and pepper

2 tablespoons chopped fresh coriander, to garnish

Curry Sauce:

3 shallots, chopped

2 fresh red chillies, deseeded and chopped

3 tablespoons desiccated coconut

½ teaspoon fennel seeds, lightly crushed

3 tablespoons vegetable oil

1 tablespoon ground coriander

1 teaspoon ground cumin

½ teaspoon chilli powder

250 g/8 oz ripe tomatoes, roughly chopped

¼ teaspoon salt

1 teaspoon lemon juice

4 Stir in the tomatoes, salt, lemon juice and 300 ml/½ pint water. Bring the curry sauce to the boil, then reduce the heat and simmer for about 10 minutes. Taste and adjust the seasoning if necessary.

5 Just before serving, cut the omelette into thick strips and add it to the curry sauce. Heat gently for a further 3–4 minutes then serve the curry at once, garnished with coriander.

- Serves 4
- Preparation time: 10 minutes
- Cooking time: 30 minutes

64

Cashew Nut Curry

In Sri Lanka, this curry is traditionally made from freshly picked cashew nuts. Raw cashews, soaked overnight, make a good substitute for the very fresh nuts. It is illustrated on pages 62–63.

Variation

Coriander Omelette Curry

1 Prepare the curry sauce as described in the main recipe and set it aside while preparing the omelette.

2 Beat together 4 eggs, 3 shallots, finely chopped, 1 large fresh red chilli, deseeded and finely chopped, 4 tablespoons chopped fresh coriander, 1 teaspoon lemon juice and plenty of salt and pepper.

3 Heat 1 tablespoon vegetable oil in a heavy-based frying pan, pour in the egg mixture and cook over a medium heat for 5 minutes. Place the omelette pan under a preheated grill and cook the top of the omelette for a further 5 minutes.

4 Remove the omelette from the pan and cut it into thick strips. Add the omelette to the curry sauce and heat through gently for 3–4 minutes. Serve at once, garnished with sprigs of coriander and shredded fresh red chilli.

- Serves 4
- Preparation time: 10 minutes
- Cooking time: 30 minutes

1 Place all the ingredients except the cashew nuts and the creamed coconut in a heavy-based saucepan. Stir everything together to combine, bring the mixture to the boil, then reduce the heat and simmer gently, leaving the pan uncovered, for 15 minutes or until the sauce has thickened slightly.

2 Drain the cashew nuts and add them to the pan. Cook over a gentle heat, stirring occasionally, for 20 minutes, or until the nuts are tender.

3 Add the chopped creamed coconut to the pan, stir well to allow it to dissolve and simmer the curry gently for a further 5 minutes, without letting it boil. Taste and adjust the seasoning if necessary. Serve immediately.

600 ml/1 pint thin coconut milk

3 shallots, thinly sliced

1 stalk of lemon grass, halved lengthways

5 curry leaves

2 garlic cloves, crushed

2 large fresh red chillies halved lengthways, deseeded and thinly sliced

1 tablespoon grated fresh root ginger

1 teaspoon black mustard seeds

½ teaspoon turmeric

½ teaspoon chilli powder

¼ teaspoon ground cinnamon

1 teaspoon salt

250 g/8 oz raw cashew nuts, soaked overnight in cold water

25 g/1 oz creamed coconut, finely chopped

- Serves 4–6
- Preparation time: 10 minutes, plus overnight soaking
- Cooking time: 45 minutes

Ceylon Beef Curry

1 Heat the ghee in a heavy-based saucepan, add the onion, garlic and ginger, and fry over a low heat, stirring frequently, for 5 minutes until softened.

2 Add the curry powder, turmeric and mustard seeds and fry over a low heat, stirring constantly, for a further 2 minutes until aromatic.

3 Stir in the salt, vinegar, chillies, tomatoes and beef and mix well to coat the beef, evenly in the spices.

4 Cover the pan and cook the curry over a low heat, stirring occasionally, for 50 minutes or until the meat is very tender.

5 Remove the lid, stir in the sugar and cook the curry uncovered for a further 10 minutes, stirring occasionally, until the sauce is thick. Taste and adjust the seasoning if necessary and serve immediately. Sri Lankan yellow rice (see page 102) would be a good accompaniment to this curry.

- Serves 4
- Preparation time: about 15 minutes
- Cooking time: 1¼ hours

2 tablespoons ghee

1 large onion, thinly sliced

3 garlic cloves, crushed

2.5 cm/1 inch piece of fresh root ginger, finely chopped

2 tablespoons Sri Lankan curry powder (see page 116)

1 teaspoon turmeric

1 tablespoon mustard seeds

1 teaspoon salt

1 tablespoon white wine vinegar

2 fresh red chillies, deseeded and thinly sliced

4 tomatoes (approximate weight 275 g/9 oz), chopped

625 g/1¼ lb fillet of beef, cut into 5 cm/2 inch cubes

1 teaspoon soft brown sugar

Galle Fried Squid Curry

If liked the squid tentacles can also be cooked in this curry – it is purely a matter of taste whether or not they are included. It is illustrated opposite.

1 Place all the ingredients for the curry sauce in a heavy-based saucepan, season with salt and bring to the boil. Then reduce the heat and simmer the sauce for about 45 minutes until it is very thick.

2 Heat half the oil in a large frying pan and add half the squid. Cook it over a fairly high heat, stirring constantly, for 1–2 minutes or until the squid has turned white and is just cooked. Using a slotted spoon, transfer the squid to the curry sauce and repeat the process with the remaining oil and squid. (If the tentacles are to be cooked they will take about 2 minutes and will be tinged with pink when they are done.)

3 Stir the sugar into the squid curry and simmer the curry gently for 5 minutes to heat through. Taste and adjust the seasoning if necessary and serve at once, garnished with curry leaves, if using.

- Serves 4–6
- Preparation time: about 20 minutes
- Cooking time: 1 hour

3 tablespoons vegetable oil

1 kg/2 lb small squid, cleaned and cut into 2.5 cm/1 inch rings

1 teaspoon soft brown sugar

fresh curry leaves, to garnish (optional)

Curry Sauce:

2 small onions, finely chopped

3 garlic cloves, crushed

8 curry leaves

7 cm/3 inch piece of cinnamon stick, broken in half

1 stalk of lemon grass, bruised

½ teaspoon ginger

1 teaspoon turmeric

1 teaspoon chilli powder

1 tablespoon Sri Lankan curry powder (see page 116)

3 tablespoons lime juice

600 ml/1 pint coconut milk

salt

66

Aubergine Pahi

This pickled aubergine dish is a favourite in many Sri Lankan households. It can be stored in the refrigerator for about a week as the vinegar acts as a preservative.

1 Mix together the salt and turmeric and rub all over the sliced aubergines. Leave to drain for 2 hours.

2 Place the ingredients for the spice paste in a blender or food processor and blend to produce a thick paste. Set aside.

3 Place the coriander, cumin and fennel seeds in a pan and dry-fry, stirring, for 3 minutes until fragrant. Leave to cool.

4 Pat the aubergine slices dry on kitchen paper. Heat about 1 cm/½ inch oil in a heavy-based frying pan and cook the aubergine slices, in batches, in the hot oil for about 2 minutes on each side until crisp and golden. Remove with a slotted spoon, drain on kitchen paper.

5 Drain off all but 4 tablespoons of the oil and add the spice paste to the pan. Cook over a gentle heat for 5 minutes, stirring occasionally. Add the dry-fried spices, chillies, paprika and cinnamon. Cook, stirring, for 2 minutes more.

7 Add the aubergine and 175 ml/6 fl oz water. Cover and cook for 15–20 minutes, stirring. Stir in the sugar and serve.

2 teaspoons salt

2 teaspoons turmeric

500 g/1 lb aubergines, very thinly sliced

1 tablespoon ground coriander

1 tablespoon ground cumin

½ teaspoon fennel seeds, crushed

vegetable oil

3 fresh red chillies, deseeded and chopped

1 teaspoon paprika

½ teaspoon ground cinnamon

1 tablespoon caster sugar

Blended Spice Paste:

1 onion, chopped

3 garlic cloves, chopped

2.5 cm/1 inch piece of fresh root ginger, chopped

1 tablespoon black mustard seeds

150 ml/¼ pint malt vinegar

- Serves 4
- Preparation time: 15–20 minutes, plus 2 hours draining time
- Cooking time: 45 minutes

Sri Lankan Fried Pork Curry

This type of curry is called Badun in Sri Lanka – it is rich, dark and full of flavour.

1 Heat 2 tablespoons of the oil in a heavy-based saucepan, add the fenugreek and curry leaves and fry gently for 2 minutes.

2 Place the onion, garlic and ginger in a blender or food processor and blend to a paste. Add to the pan and fry, stirring occasionally for 5 minutes.

3 Add the curry powder, chilli powder, salt, vinegar and pork. Mix well and then increase the heat and cook, stirring frequently for 8 minutes.

3 Stir in the cinnamon, cardamom, sugar and 150 ml/¼ pint water, cover and simmer gently for 30 minutes, stirring occasionally.

4 Stir in the coconut milk and increase the heat. Cook uncovered for a further 10 minutes, stirring frequently.

5 Using a slotted spoon, remove the pieces of pork from the sauce. Heat the remaining oil in a heavy-based frying pan and add the pork. Fry the pork, turning it frequently for 8 minutes or until it is browned all over.

6 Drain off the oil and return the fried pork to the sauce. Simmer for 10 minutes more or until you have a dark sauce. Serve hot garnished with coconut shreds, if using.

4 tablespoons vegetable oil

¼ teaspoon fenugreek seeds

5 curry leaves

1 large onion, chopped

3 garlic cloves, crushed

2.5 cm/1 inch piece of fresh root ginger, chopped

2 tablespoons Sri Lankan curry powder (see page 116)

1 teaspoon chilli powder

1 teaspoon salt

3 tablespoons malt vinegar

625 g/1¼ lb pork tenderloin, cut into 5 cm/2 inch pieces

2.5 cm/1 inch piece cinnamon stick

4 cardamom pods, bruised

1 teaspoon soft brown sugar

300 ml/½ pint coconut milk

fresh coconut shreds, to garnish (optional)

- Serves 4–6
- Preparation time: 30 minutes
- Cooking time: 1 hour

68

Duck Padre Curry

The origins of this Sri Lankan curry's name remain a mystery. One suggestion is that the recipe's use of whisky might allow a seemingly abstemious vicar a surreptitious tot (or sip) of his favourite tipple!

1 Trim away any excess fat from the duck legs and place them in a large, heavy-based saucepan. Add the onion, garlic, ginger, lemon grass, curry leaves, cinnamon, salt, vinegar and coconut milk, and stir to mix all the ingredients.

2 Dry-roast the ingredients for the roasted spice mix in a small frying pan for 2 minutes until fragrant, then grind them to a powder in a spice mill or with a pestle and mortar. Stir the ground spices into the pan with the duck, bring the curry to the boil, then reduce the heat, cover and simmer gently for 1 hour, stirring occasionally, until the duck is tender. After 1 hour, remove the lid and cook the curry uncovered for a further 15 minutes.

3 Stir the whisky and sugar into the curry and simmer it for a further 15 minutes. Taste and adjust the seasoning if necessary and serve immediately.

- Serves 4
- Preparation time: 10 minutes
- Cooking time: 1½–1¾ hours

4 duck legs, about 175 g/ 6 oz each

1 large onion, chopped

4 garlic cloves, finely chopped

1 tablespoon grated fresh root ginger

1 stalk of lemon grass, halved lengthways

4 curry leaves

½ teaspoon ground cinnamon

1 teaspoon salt

50 ml/2 fl oz distilled malt vinegar

300 ml/½ pint coconut milk

50 ml/2 fl oz whisky

2 teaspoons soft brown sugar or according to taste

Roasted Spice Mix:

6 dried red chillies

2 teaspoons cumin seeds

2 teaspoons coriander seeds

Variation

Pork Padre Curry

1 Use the same ingredients as for the main recipe, replacing the duck with 625 g/1¼ lb pork tenderloin cut into 1.5 cm/ ¾ inch slices.

2 Cook the pork curry for 1 hour, then simmer uncovered for only 10 minutes before and 10 minutes after the addition of the whisky.

3 Serve the pork curry with fried sliced potatoes, made by thinly slicing 375 g/12 oz cooked potatoes and frying them in 2 batches in 3 tablespoons ghee for 5–7 minutes on each side, until they are crisp and golden. Drain on kitchen paper and sprinkle with salt.

- Serves 4
- Preparation time: 30 minutes
- Cooking time: about 1½ hours

Thailand, Burma and Indochina

Moving east, away from India, new herbs and spice blends appear in the curries of Burma, Thailand, Laos, Cambodia and Vietnam. The fresh, citrus flavours of lime leaves and lemon grass and the tang of pungent fish sauce seem to give a lighter feel to these curries, but they can also be fiercely hot, depending on the amount of chillies used in the sauce.

Siamese Pineapple and Mussel Curry

The spiciness of this dish will depend on the type of curry paste used. Shop-bought curry pastes are generally more fiery than the homemade one I have suggested here, for which I have given the recipe on page 118. It is illustrated on pages 70–71.

1 Scrub the mussels with a stiff brush and scrape off the beards and barnacles with a sharp knife. Wash well in cold water and discard any open mussels.

2 Pour about 2.5 cm/1 inch of water into a large saucepan, add the chopped lemon grass and Thai basil and bring the water to the boil. Tip in the mussels, cover the pan and steam the mussels for 3–4 minutes or until they have opened and are cooked. Drain the mussels, discarding the lemon grass, Thai basil and any mussels which have not opened Set the mussels aside while preparing the sauce.

3 Heat the oil in a heavy-based saucepan, add the curry paste, galangal, chilli and lime leaves and fry over a gentle heat, stirring for about 4 minutes, until fragrant. Stir in the coconut milk, fish sauce and sugar and cook for a further minute.

4 Reserve a few mussels in their shells for garnish and remove the remaining mussels from their shells. Add the shelled mussels and pineapple to the curry sauce. Stir gently and cook for 2–3 minutes to heat through. Serve hot, garnished with the reserved mussels and Thai basil, if using.

- Serves 4
- Preparation time: 30 minutes
- Cooking time: 10–15 minutes

1 kg/2 lb fresh mussels

2 stalks of lemon grass, roughly chopped

20 Thai basil leaves

2 tablespoons groundnut oil

2 tablespoons Thai red curry paste (see page 118)

5 cm/2 inch piece of fresh galangal finely chopped

1 large green chilli, thinly sliced

4 Kaffir lime leaves, finely chopped

200 ml/7 fl oz coconut milk

1 tablespoon fish sauce

1 teaspoon palm sugar or soft brown sugar

175 g/6 oz peeled fresh pineapple, cut into bite-sized pieces

Thai basil leaves, to garnish (optional)

Thai Yellow Prawn Curry

1 Place the ingredients for the curry paste in a blender or food processor and blend to produce a thick paste. Heat the oil in a wok or saucepan, add the curry paste and fry over a gentle heat, stirring for 4 minutes, until the paste is fragrant. Stir the 125 ml/4 fl oz water into the curry paste, bring to the boil and cook over a fairly high heat for 2 minutes to evaporate some of the water.

2 Stir the coconut milk into the curry paste and then add the prawns. Cook the curry over a medium heat, stirring occasionally, for about 6 minutes or until the prawns have turned pink and are cooked through.

3 Stir in the fish sauce and lime juice, and taste and adjust the seasoning, if necessary. Transfer the curry to a warmed serving dish, garnished with the spring onions and chilli and serve immediately.

- Serves 4
- Preparation time: 10 minutes
- Cooking time: 15 minutes

3 tablespoons groundnut oil

250 ml/8 fl oz coconut milk

20 uncooked king prawns, peeled

2 teaspoons fish sauce

1 teaspoon lime juice

Yellow Curry Paste:

2.5 cm/1 inch piece of fresh galangal, finely chopped

1 stalk of lemon grass, finely chopped

2 shallots, chopped

3 garlic cloves, chopped

2 teaspoons turmeric

1 teaspoon ground coriander

1 teaspoon ground cumin

1 teaspoon shrimp paste

½ teaspoon chilli powder

To garnish:

3 spring onions, sliced

2 fresh red chillies, shredded

Thai Red Prawn and Cucumber Curry

1 Heat the oil in a wok, add the shallot and garlic and fry over a gentle heat, stirring for about 3 minutes, until softened. Add the red curry paste, chilli and lime leaves and fry for a further 1 minute.

2 Add the coconut milk, increase the heat and bring the sauce to the boil, then reduce the heat and simmer the sauce gently, stirring occasionally, for 5 minutes.

3 Add the prawns, cucumber, fish sauce and sugar to the wok. Stir to coat the ingredients evenly in the sauce, then simmer the curry gently for 5 minutes or until the prawns have turned pink and are cooked through and the cucumber is tender. Taste and adjust the seasoning, if necessary. Serve the curry hot, garnished with chopped coriander.

2 tablespoons groundnut oil

1 shallot, chopped

2 garlic cloves, chopped

2 tablespoons Thai red curry paste (see page 118)

1 fresh red chilli, deseeded and chopped

3 Kaffir lime leaves, finely shredded

300 ml/½ pint coconut milk

20 uncooked king prawns, peeled

125 g/4 oz cucumber, peeled, halved lengthways, deseeded and sliced thickly

1 tablespoon fish sauce

1 teaspoon palm sugar or soft brown sugar

chopped coriander, to garnish

- Serves 4
- Preparation time: about 10 minutes
- Cooking time: 15 minutes

Variation

Thai Red Chicken Curry

1 Heat 2 tablespoons of groundnut oil in a wok, add 1 small onion, chopped, 1 stalk of lemon grass, chopped, and 3 tablespoons Thai red curry paste (see page 118) and fry over a gentle heat, stirring occasionally, for 3 minutes.

2 Add 625 g/1¼ lb skinless, boneless chicken breasts cut into bite-sized pieces. Stir to coat the chicken evenly in the curry paste and fry for a further 3 minutes.

3 Stir in 300 ml/½ pint coconut milk, 5 Kaffir lime leaves, finely shredded, and 2 teaspoons soft brown sugar. Bring the curry to the boil, then reduce the heat to moderate and cook the curry, stirring occasionally, for 15 minutes or until the chicken is cooked through.

4 Stir in 1 tablespoon chopped fresh Thai basil leaves, 1 tablespoon fish sauce and 50 g/2 oz salted peanuts, roughly chopped. Cook the curry for a further 3 minutes. Taste and adjust the seasoning, if necessary. Serve immediately, garnished with Thai basil leaves.

- Serves 4
- Preparation time: 10 minutes
- Cooking time: 25–30 minutes

Cambodian Prawn and Marrow Curry

Serve this curry immediately with rice or bread. It is illustrated opposite.

1 Place all the ingredients for the spice paste in a blender or food processor and blend to produce a coarse paste. Heat the oil in a large flameproof casserole, add the spice paste and fry over a gentle heat, stirring for about 8 minutes or until softened and cooked.

2 Add the coconut milk, stir well and simmer gently for 3–4 minutes. Stir the marrow into the sauce, cover the pan and cook gently for 5 minutes.

3 Add the prawns, fish sauce, lemon juice and sugar to the pan. Stir gently to combine all the ingredients and cook the curry, uncovered, for a further 5 minutes until the prawns have turned pink and are cooked through and the marrow is tender. Taste and adjust the seasoning if necessary. Garnish with coriander sprigs and serve with plain boiled rice.

3 tablespoons vegetable oil

300 ml/½ pint coconut milk

250 g/8 oz (prepared weight) young marrow, peeled, deseeded and cut into 2.5 cm/1 inch chunks

20 large uncooked prawns, peeled

2 tablespoons fish sauce

1 tablespoon lemon juice

1 teaspoon caster sugar

Spice Paste:

1 onion, chopped

4 garlic cloves, chopped

1 stalk of lemon grass, chopped

1 tablespoon chopped fresh root ginger

2 teaspoons ground coriander

1 teaspoon chilli powder

½ teaspoon turmeric

½ teaspoon fennel seeds, lightly crushed

sprigs of coriander, to garnish

- Serves 4
- Preparation time: about 25 minutes
- Cooking time: 25 minutes

Burmese Beef and Pumpkin Curry

This delicious curry is illustrated opposite.

1 Place all the ingredients for the spice paste in a blender or food processor and blend to produce a coarse paste. Heat the oil in a large flameproof casserole, add the spice paste and fry over a gentle heat, stirring for about 5 minutes or until softened. Add the chilli flakes and turmeric and fry for a further 2 minutes.

2 Add the beef to the pan, stir well to coat the beef in the spice mixture and fry, stirring frequently, for 5 minutes. Add the stock and sugar to the curry and bring it to the boil. Reduce the heat, cover the pan and cook the curry, stirring occasionally, for 35 minutes or until the beef is tender.

3 Add the pumpkin and salt to the pan, stir gently to mix, cover and cook for a further 10 minutes or until the pumpkin is tender. Taste and adjust the seasoning, if necessary. Serve the curry garnished with ginger, if liked. Steamed white rice would be a good accompaniment.

3 tablespoons sesame oil

2 teaspoons dried chilli flakes

1 teaspoon turmeric

625 g/1¼ lb sirloin steak, cut into 2.5 cm/1 inch cubes

300 ml/½ pint beef stock

1 teaspoon soft brown sugar

500 g/1 lb pumpkin, peeled and cut into 2.5 cm/1 inch cubes

½ teaspoon salt

1.5 cm/¾ inch piece of fresh root ginger, finely shredded, to garnish (optional)

Spice Paste:

2 large onions, chopped

4 garlic cloves, chopped

2 stalks of lemon grass, chopped

2.5 cm/1 inch piece of fresh root ginger, chopped

- Serves 4–6
- Preparation time: 25 minutes
- Cooking time: 50 minutes

Thai Green Chicken Curry

It is illustrated on pages 70–71.

1 Heat the oil in a wok, add the ginger and shallots and fry over a gentle heat, stirring for about 3 minutes or until softened. Add the green curry paste and fry for a further 2 minutes.

2 Add the chicken to the wok, stir to coat evenly in the spice mixture and fry for 3 minutes to seal the chicken. Stir the coconut milk into the curry, bring it to the boil, then reduce the heat and cook the curry gently, stirring occasionally, for 10 minutes or until the chicken is cooked through and the sauce has thickened.

3 Stir in the fish sauce, sugar, lime leaves and green chilli and cook the curry for a further 5 minutes. Taste and adjust the seasoning, if necessary and serve the curry immediately, garnished with Thai basil leaves, if liked.

2 tablespoons groundnut oil

2.5 cm/1 inch piece of fresh root ginger, finely chopped

2 shallots, chopped

4 tablespoons Thai green curry paste (see page 118)

625 g/1¼ lb skinless, boneless chicken thighs, cut into 5 cm/2 inch pieces

300 ml/½ pint coconut milk

4 teaspoons fish sauce

1 teaspoon palm sugar or soft brown sugar

3 Kaffir lime leaves, shredded

1 green chilli, deseeded and sliced

Thai basil leaves, to garnish (optional)

- Serves 4
- Preparation time: 10 minutes
- Cooking time: 25 minutes

Thai Steamed Fish Curry

Steaming is a delicious way of cooking fish curry. This gentle cooking process ensures moist, delicately cooked fish.

1 Mix the Thai red curry paste, coconut milk, fish sauce and beaten egg together. Set aside.

2 Place the fish pieces in a shallow non-metallic dish. Add the fresh coriander, mint and Thai basil leaves and gently mix to combine thoroughly. Pour over the curry paste mixture and stir to coat the fish evenly.

3 Scatter over the shredded lime leaves and the sliced green chilli. Cover the dish with foil and place it in a steamer above a pan of boiling water. Steam the fish for 15 minutes or until it is just cooked through. The sauce should be lightly 'set' due to the addition of the egg. Serve immediately with steamed Thai fragrant rice.

3 tablespoons Thai red curry paste (see page 118)

125 g/4 oz creamed coconut, chopped and dissolved in 200 ml/7 fl oz boiling water

1 tablespoon fish sauce

1 egg, beaten

500 g/1 lb skinless seabass fillets, cut into 5 cm/2 inch pieces

1 tablespoon torn fresh coriander leaves

1 tablespoon torn fresh mint leaves

1 tablespoon torn fresh Thai basil leaves

4 Kaffir lime leaves, finely shredded

1 large green chilli, deseeded and thinly sliced

- Serves 4
- Preparation time: 10 minutes
- Cooking time: 15 minutes

76

Phuket Chicken and Lemon Grass Curry

1 Heat the oil in a large flame-proof casserole, add the garlic and shallots, and fry over a gentle heat, stirring, for 3 minutes or until softened.

2 Add the lemon grass, lime leaves, green curry paste, fish sauce and sugar to the pan. Fry for 1 minute, then add the stock and chicken drumsticks and bring the curry to the boil. Reduce the heat, cover the pan and simmer the curry gently, stirring occasionally, for 40–45 minutes, until the chicken is tender and cooked through.

3 Taste and adjust the seasoning if necessary. Serve the curry hot, garnished with lime leaves. Plain boiled rice would be a good accompaniment to this curry.

- Serves 4
- Preparation time: 15 minutes
- Cooking time: 50 minutes

3 tablespoons vegetable oil

4 garlic cloves, crushed

3 shallots, chopped

3 stalks of lemon grass, very finely chopped

6 Kaffir lime leaves, shredded

3 tablespoons Thai green curry paste (see page 118)

1 tablespoon fish sauce

2 teaspoons palm sugar or soft brown sugar

250 ml/8 fl oz chicken stock

8 large chicken drumsticks

Kaffir lime leaves, to garnish

Chiang Mai Jungle Curry with Beef

The fiery flavours of this curry are typical of northern Thailand. Jungle dishes from that area often contain exotic meats such as monkey or snake but I have settled for beef in this version!

1 Place the ingredients for the spice paste in a food processor or blender and process to produce a thick paste. Heat the oil in a large flameproof casserole, add the beef and fry over a moderate heat, stirring, for 3 minutes to seal the meat. Stir in the spice paste and fry for a further 3 minutes.

2 Add the coconut milk to the pan, stir to mix and bring the curry to the boil, then reduce the heat, cover the pan and simmer the curry gently, stirring occasionally, for 50 minutes or until the beef is tender. Taste and adjust the seasoning if necessary.

3 Serve the curry hot, garnished with slices of lime. Jasmine rice would make a good accompaniment.

- Serves 4
- Preparation time: 15 minutes
- Cooking time: 1 hour

2 tablespoons groundnut oil

500 g/1 lb lean beef, e.g. rump or sirloin steak, cut into thin slices

400 ml/14 fl oz coconut milk

lime slices, to garnish

Spice Paste:

2 tablespoons yellow bean sauce

3 tablespoons Thai red curry paste (see page 118)

2 tablespoons soft brown sugar

4 shallots, chopped

2 garlic cloves, chopped

2 large fresh red chillies, deseeded and chopped

1 stalk of lemon grass, chopped

2.5 cm/1 inch piece of fresh galangal, chopped

½ teaspoon shrimp paste

juice of 2 limes

77

Burmese Chicken Curry and Cellophane Noodles

This traditional Burmese dish, illustrated opposite, is served with noodles. It is the ideal dish for an informal dinner party, as with its accompaniments, it is a meal in itself.

1 Start by preparing the curry. Place all the ingredients for the spice paste in a blender or food processor and blend to produce a thick paste. Heat the groundnut oil in a large heavy-based saucepan, add the spice paste and fry over a gentle heat, stirring constantly for 5 minutes until softened.

2 Add the chicken pieces and fry, stirring constantly, for a further 5 minutes to seal. Stir in the chilli powder, turmeric, salt, coconut milk and stock. Bring the curry to the boil, then reduce the heat and simmer very gently, stirring occasionally, for 30 minutes or until the chicken is tender.

3 Stir the creamed coconut into the curry and then simmer over a medium heat for 2–3 minutes, stirring the mixture constantly, until the creamed coconut has dissolved and thickened the sauce slightly. Taste and adjust the seasoning if necessary.

4 Drop the dried noodles into a pan of salted boiling water. Bring the water back to the boil and cook the noodles for 3 minutes. Drain the noodles and stir through a little sesame oil.

5 To serve, divide the noodles between 4 deep soup bowls and ladle some chicken curry over each portion. Serve the accompaniments separately. The fried dried chillies should be nibbled at with caution: they are extremely hot!

- Serves 4
- Preparation time: 15 minutes
- Cooking time: 50 minutes

4 tablespoons groundnut oil

625 g/1¼ lb skinless, boneless chicken breasts, cut into bite-sized pieces

1½ teaspoons chilli powder

½ teaspoon turmeric

½ teaspoon salt

600 ml/1 pint coconut milk

300 ml/½ pint chicken stock

50 g/2 oz creamed coconut, chopped

375 g/12 oz cellophane noodles

sesame oil

salt

Spice Paste:

4 large garlic cloves, chopped

2 onions, chopped

1 large fresh red chilli, deseeded and chopped

2.5 cm/1 inch piece of fresh root ginger, chopped

1 teaspoon shrimp paste

Accompaniments:

3 spring onions, sliced

2 tablespoons crisply fried onion flakes

3 garlic cloves, sliced and crisply fried

2 tablespoons fresh coriander leaves

1 lemon, cut into wedges

whole dried chillies, fried (optional)

Thai Pork Curry

1 Place all the ingredients for the curry paste in a blender or food processor and blend to produce a thick paste.

2 Heat the oil in a heavy-based saucepan, add the shallots and chilli and fry over a gentle heat, stirring, for 3 minutes. Stir in the curry paste and fry for a further 1 minute.

3 Add the pork to the pan, stir to coat it evenly in the spice mixture then stir in the fish sauce and brown sugar. Cook, stirring, for 3 minutes. Add the coconut milk to the pan, bring the curry to the boil then lower the heat and simmer gently for 20 minutes, stirring just occasionally, until the pork is tender.

4 Stir in the bamboo shoots and coriander. Cook for 2 minutes, to heat through. Serve hot, garnished with chilli rings. Steamed jasmine rice is a good accompaniment to this curry.

2 tablespoons groundnut oil

2 shallots, sliced

1 green chilli, deseeded and sliced

500 g/1 lb pork tenderloin, cut into bite-sized pieces

1 tablespoon fish sauce

½ teaspoon soft brown sugar

150 ml/¼ pint coconut milk

75 g/3 oz canned bamboo shoots, drained

2 tablespoons chopped fresh coriander

1 green chilli, cut into rings, to garnish

Curry Paste:

2 large dried red chillies, deseeded and chopped

3 garlic cloves, crushed

2 Kaffir lime leaves, chopped

6 black peppercorns, crushed

1 tablespoon chopped lemon grass

½ teaspoon shrimp paste

- Serves 4
- Preparation time: 25 minutes
- Cooking time: 30 minutes

Burmese Prawn Kebab Curry

1 Prepare the prawn kebabs. Thread 2 prawns, 1 slice of garlic, 1 chunk of red chilli, ½ a shallot and 1 slice of ginger on to each cocktail stick. Set aside while preparing the sauce.

2 Place the onion and garlic in a blender or food processor and blend to a coarse paste. Heat the oil in a saucepan, add the paste and fry, stirring frequently, for 5 minutes until golden.

3 Add the turmeric, chilli powder and ground coriander, stir and fry for a further minute. Stir in the salt and fish stock, bring to the boil, then cover the pan and simmer gently, stirring occasionally, for 20 minutes.

4 Add the prawn kebabs to the curry sauce, cover and cook for a further 7–8 minutes to cook the kebabs. Remove the kebabs and keep them warm.

5 Increase the heat to medium and cook the sauce, uncovered, for 6–8 minutes to thicken it. Stir in the chopped coriander. Pour the sauce over the kebabs, garnish with coriander and chilli, and serve with rice.

32 peeled medium prawns, uncooked weighing about 15 g/½ oz each

4 large garlic cloves, cut into 16 thin slices

2 large fresh red chillies, each deseeded and cut each into 16 chunks

8 shallots, halved lengthways

2.5 cm/1 inch piece of fresh root ginger, cut into 16 thin slices

16 cocktail sticks

Curry Sauce:

1 large onion, chopped

4 garlic cloves, chopped

2 tablespoons vegetable oil

1 teaspoon turmeric

½ teaspoon chilli powder

½ teaspoon ground coriander

¼ teaspoon salt

600 ml/1 pint fish stock

2 tablespoons chopped fresh coriander

To garnish:

sprigs of coriander

1 fresh red chilli, sliced

- Serves 4
- Preparation time: 10 minutes
- Cooking time: 45 minutes

Burmese Pork Curry

1 Heat the ghee in a heavy-based saucepan, add the onion, garlic, ginger and pork, and fry over a brisk heat, stirring constantly, for 4 minutes until lightly golden.

2 Lower the heat, stir in the turmeric, sugar, curry paste, shrimp paste, dried chillies and lemon grass, and fry for a further 2 minutes.

3 Add the stock and soy sauce to the pan, stir to mix well, then bring the curry to the boil. Cover the pan, reduce the heat and cook the curry gently for 30 minutes, stirring occasionally, until the pork is tender. Discard the stalks of lemon grass and taste and adjust the seasoning, if necessary. Serve the curry hot garnished with sliced red chillies.

- Serves 4
- Preparation time: 10 minutes
- Cooking time: 45 minutes

2 tablespoons ghee

2 small onions, each cut into 8 wedges

4 garlic cloves, finely chopped

5 cm/2 inch piece of fresh root ginger, finely chopped

500 g/1 lb pork tenderloin, cut into 2.5 cm/1 inch cubes

1 teaspoon turmeric

½ teaspoon soft brown sugar

1 tablespoon mild curry paste

1 teaspoon shrimp paste

4 dried chillies, soaked in cold water for 10 minutes, then drained and finely chopped

2 stalks of lemon grass, quartered lengthways

150 ml/¼ pint vegetable stock

2 teaspoons soy sauce

2 fresh red chillies, thinly sliced, to garnish

Vietnamese Chicken and Sweet Potato Curry

This is a delicious curry with a sweet flavour due to the addition of the sweet potato.

1 Place all the ingredients for the blended paste in a food processor and blend to produce a thick paste. Set aside.

2 Cook the potato in a pan of boiling, salted water for 8–10 minutes until it is tender. Drain and set it aside.

3 Heat the oil in a wok. Add the paste and fry over a gentle heat, stirring for about 5 minutes, until softened but not coloured. Stir in the curry powder, turmeric and chilli flakes and fry for a further 2 minutes.

4 Add the chicken to the wok, stir to coat it evenly in the spice mixture and fry, stirring, for 2 minutes. Add the stock bring it to the boil, then reduce the heat and simmer gently for 10 minutes or until most of the stock has evaporated. Stir in the coconut milk, salt and pepper and cook the curry gently, stirring occasionally, for a further 10 minutes. Stir the cooked sweet potato into the curry and heat through for 3–4 minutes. Taste and adjust the seasoning if necessary. Serve the curry garnished with spring onion slices. Steamed rice would be a good accompaniment to this dish.

- Serves 4–6
- Preparation time: 15 minutes
- Cooking time: 45 minutes

4 tablespoons groundnut oil

500 g/1 lb sweet potato, peeled and cut into 2.5 cm/1 inch chunks

1 tablespoon hot curry powder

1 teaspoon turmeric

1 teaspoon dried chilli flakes

500 g/1 lb skinless, boneless chicken breasts, cut into bite-sized pieces

300 ml/½ pint chicken stock

150 ml/¼ pint coconut milk

½ teaspoon salt

ground black pepper

3 spring onions, cut into julienne slices, to garnish

Blended Paste:

1 large onion, chopped roughly

3 garlic cloves, chopped

1 stalk of lemon grass, chopped finely

81

Malaysia

The distinctive sour flavour of tamarind and the pungency of shrimp paste are just two examples of the exotic ingredients typical of Malaysian curries. Coconut milk forms the basis of many rich, spicy dishes, and another feature of everyday Malaysian food is the combination of curry and noodles – the perfect one-dish meal.

Assam Fish Curry

Assam means sour in Malay and usually implies that tamarind pulp is used in the cooking, for its distinctive, tangy flavour. It is illustrated on pages 82–83.

1 Place the ingredients for the spice paste in a blender or food processor and blend to produce a thick paste. Heat the oil in a large saucepan, add the paste and fry over a gentle heat, stirring constantly, for about 5 minutes until softened.

2 Strain the tamarind pulp through a sieve, pressing it against the sieve to extract as much tamarind flavour as possible. Discard the pulp and add the strained tamarind liquid to the pan with the tomatoes, aubergines and chillies. Bring to the boil, then reduce the heat, cover the pan and simmer gently for 12 minutes.

3 Add the sugar, salt and prepared fish to the pan and stir gently to coat the fish in the sauce. Cover the pan and cook the curry over a gentle heat for a further 7 minutes or until the fish is cooked through. Taste and adjust the seasoning if necessary. Serve the curry hot with plain boiled rice.

- Serves 4
- Preparation time: about 20 minutes, plus soaking time
- Cooking time: 25–30 minutes

4 tablespoons vegetable oil

3 tablespoons tamarind pulp, soaked in 250 ml/ 8 fl oz boiling water for 10 minutes

2 tomatoes, quartered

2 baby aubergines, weighing about 50 g/2 oz each, quartered

2 large fresh red chillies, quartered lengthways and deseeded

1 tablespoon soft brown sugar

½ teaspoon salt

625 g/1¼ lb skinless haddock or halibut, cut into 5 cm/2 inch pieces

Spice Paste:

5 small dried chillies soaked in cold water for 10 minutes, then deseeded and chopped

8 shallots, chopped

3 stalks of lemon grass, chopped

2 fresh red chillies, deseeded and chopped

2.5 cm/1 inch piece of fresh galangal, chopped

2 teaspoons dried shrimp paste

1 teaspoon turmeric

5 candlenuts or macadamia nuts (optional)

Variation

Assam Squid Curry

1 For this variation, use the same ingredients as in the main recipe replacing the fish with 375 g/12 oz cleaned, small squid, left whole.

2 Follow the method of the main recipe until the final stage when the squid is added to the pan. Cook the squid for only 5 minutes, leaving the pan uncovered at this stage.

- Serves 4
- Preparation time: about 20 minutes, plus 20 minutes soaking time
- Cooking time: 25 minutes

Nonya Prawn and Pineapple Curry

This delicious recipe is illustrated on pages 82–83.

1 Place the ingredients for the spice paste in a food processor or blender and blend to produce a thick paste. Heat the oil in a wok, add the paste and fry over a gentle heat, stirring constantly, for 5 minutes until softened and fragrant.

2 Add half of the thin coconut milk, stir well and then bring it to simmering point. Cook for about 3 minutes until the sauce has thickened, then stir in the remaining thin coconut milk and cook for 2 minutes more.

3 Add the pineapple and salt to the curry sauce. Cook, stirring, for 2 minutes. Add the prawns and cook for a further 5 minutes until the prawns have turned pink.

4 Stir the thick coconut milk into the curry and simmer very gently for 2 minutes to heat it through. Taste and adjust the seasoning if necessary. Serve hot, garnished with coriander and pineapple. Steamed rice would be a good accompaniment to this dish.

5 tablespoons vegetable oil

250 g/8 oz peeled fresh pineapple, cut into chunks

1 teaspoon salt

20 large uncooked prawns, peeled with tails left intact

Spice Paste:

2 tablespoons coriander seeds, lightly crushed

2 tablespoons chopped fresh coriander

1 tablespoon turmeric

½ teaspoon shrimp paste

1 stalk of lemon grass, chopped

5 shallots, chopped

3 garlic cloves, chopped

3 fresh red chillies, deseeded and chopped

5 small dried red chillies, soaked in cold water for 10 minutes, then deseeded and chopped

Thin Coconut Milk:

50 g/2 oz creamed coconut dissolved in 450 ml/¾ pint boiling water

Thick Coconut Milk:

25 g/1 oz creamed coconut dissolved in 50 ml/2 fl oz boiling water

To garnish:

sprigs of coriander

fresh pineapple, cut into wedges

- Serves 4
- Preparation time: 25 minutes
- Cooking time: 20 minutes

Tamil Mee

To be truly authentic, this typical street-vendor's spiced noodle dish should be cooked in single portions.

1 Place the noodles in a bowl and pour boiling water over them. Allow to stand for 4–5 minutes, then drain and set aside. Blanch the bean sprouts in boiling water for 30 seconds, then drain and set aside.

2 Place the cooked potato in a bowl, add the chilli powder, turmeric and curry paste, and mix to coat the potato evenly in the spices. Set aside.

3 Heat the oil in a wok, add the noodles and bean sprouts, and stir-fry for 1 minute. Add the vinegar, 1 teaspoon of the soy sauce and the fishcake, stir-fry for a further 1 minute. Add the potato, the diced tomato and 3 tablespoons of water and stir-fry for 2 minutes.

4 Add the tomato and chilli sauces, and cook for a further 1 minute. Beat the egg with the remaining soy sauce. Push the noodles to one side of the wok and pour in the egg mixture. Cook, stirring, for a few seconds to break up the egg. When it is half cooked, stir in the noodles and cook for a further minute, so the egg cooks and coats the noodles. Serve hot, garnished with crisply fried onions and red chilli rings.

175 g/6 oz fresh yellow noodles

50 g/2 oz bean sprouts

125 g/4 oz potato, cooked and cut into small chunks

½ teaspoon chilli powder

½ teaspoon turmeric

1 teaspoon medium-hot curry paste

1½ tablespoons vegetable oil

2 teaspoons distilled malt vinegar

1½ teaspoons dark soy sauce

50 g/2 oz Asian fishcake, thinly sliced

50 g/2 oz tomato, diced

1 tablespoon tomato sauce

1 tablespoon sweet chilli sauce

1 egg

To garnish:

½ onion, sliced and crisply fried

1 red chilli, cut into rings

- Serves 1 as a main course, 2 as a light lunch
- Preparation time: 10 minutes
- Cooking time: 15 minutes

Laksa

The English translation of this dish is Rice Noodles with Curried Chicken Soup and is basically a meal in itself. It is best served at once. This dish is illustrated opposite.

1 Heat 2 tablespoons of the oil in a wok. Fry the beancurd in the oil, in 2 batches, turning it frequently. Cook each batch for 5 minutes, until crisp and golden, then remove with a slotted spoon, drain on kitchen paper and set aside.

2 Heat 2 more tablespoons of oil in the wok, add the onions and garlic and fry over a gentle heat, stirring frequently for 5 minutes until softened.

3 Add the Brazil nuts, the ground cumin, coriander and turmeric, the red and green chillies and the shrimp and curry pastes to the wok. Stir well to mix and fry for a further 2 minutes.

4 Stir in the coconut milk and sugar and season generously with salt and pepper. Bring the curried coconut milk to the boil, then reduce the heat and simmer gently for 6 minutes. Taste and adjust the seasoning if necessary.

5 Heat the remaining oil in a frying pan, add the chicken and stir-fry for 6 minutes, until golden. Add the bean sprouts and chopped coriander and stir-fry for a further 1 minute.

6 tablespoons vegetable oil
250 g/8 oz pressed beancurd, cubed
2 red onions, finely chopped
3 garlic cloves, finely chopped
4 Brazil nuts, finely grated
2 teaspoons ground cumin
1 tablespoon ground coriander
½ teaspoon turmeric
1 red chilli, deseeded and chopped
1 green chilli, deseeded and chopped
½ teaspoon shrimp paste
2 tablespoons Thai red curry paste (see page 118)
1 litre/1¾ pints coconut milk
1 tablespoon soft brown sugar
375 g/12 oz cooked chicken breasts, shredded
125 g/4 oz bean sprouts
1 tablespoon chopped fresh coriander
250 g/8 oz dried rice vermicelli or noodles
salt and pepper

To garnish:
1 onion, sliced and crisply fried
2 fresh red chillies, chopped
fresh coriander leaves
3 spring onions, sliced

6 Place the noodles in a bowl and pour boiling water over them to cover completely. Allow the noodles to stand for 5 minutes, then drain them well.

7 To serve, divide the noodles between 4 large soup bowls. Place a quarter of the fried beancurd and a quarter of the chicken and bean sprout mixture on top of each portion of noodles. Ladle hot curry sauce over the noodles and scatter over the suggested garnishes. Serve immediately.

- Serves 4
- Preparation time: about 20 minutes
- Cooking time: 40 minutes

Nonya Aubergine and Prawn Curry

The Nonyas of Malaysia are descended from Chinese traders who intermarried with the indigenous Malays and settled in coastal areas such as Penang, Malacca and Singapore (where they are known as Peranakan). Their cooking is a distinctive blend of Chinese and Malay influences.

1 Place the ingredients for the curry paste in a blender or food processor and blend to produce a thick paste. Heat the oil in a large saucepan, add the curry paste and fry over a gentle heat, stirring constantly, for 5 minutes or until fragrant.

2 Add the coconut milk, stir well and bring to the boil, then reduce the heat and simmer gently for 3 minutes to thicken the sauce slightly.

3 Add the aubergines and the salt, stir gently to mix, then cover the pan and simmer gently, stirring occasionally, for 10 minutes or until the aubergines are tender. Stir the prawns into the curry and cook for a further 5 minutes, until the prawns have turned pink and are cooked through. Taste and adjust the seasoning if necessary and serve the curry hot with plain boiled rice.

3 tablespoons groundnut oil

300 ml/½ pint coconut milk

375 g/12 oz small aubergines, cut into 5 mm/¼ inch slices

¼ teaspoon salt

300 g/10 oz large raw prawns, peeled

Curry Paste:

5 shallots, chopped

4 large garlic cloves, chopped

3 large red chillies, deseeded and chopped

1 teaspoon shrimp paste

1 teaspoon turmeric

½ teaspoon salt

- Serves 4
- Preparation time: 10 minutes
- Cooking time: 25 minutes

Variation

Nonya Dried Prawn and Green Bean Curry

Dried prawns are available from oriental supermarkets. They are very salty, so no additional salt is needed.

1 Soak 75 g/3 oz dried prawns in cold water for 1 hour before using them. Drain and set aside.

2 Prepare the curry paste as described in the main recipe. Follow Steps 1 and 2 to create the coconut curry sauce.

3 Add 250 g/8 oz green beans, cut into 2.5 cm/1 inch lengths, and the drained prawns, cover the pan, and simmer the curry gently for 15–18 minutes, until the beans are cooked and the prawns are tender. Serve immediately, with plain boiled rice.

- Serves 4
- Preparation time: 10 minutes, plus 1 hour soaking time
- Cooking time: 25–30 minutes

Beef and Potato Curry

I Heat the oil in a saucepan, add the shallots, garlic and ginger, and fry over a gentle heat, stirring frequently, for 5 minutes or until softened. Add the curry powder, ground cinnamon, cumin, coriander, cardamom, curry leaves, star anise and whole cloves, and fry for a further 1 minute.

2 Add the beef and stir well to coat it in the spice mixture. Add the potatoes, chillies, salt and coconut milk. Stir to combine, bring to the boil, then reduce the heat, cover the pan and simmer gently, stirring occasionally, for 40 minutes until the beef is tender and the potatoes are cooked.

3 Stir in the lime juice and sugar and cook uncovered for a further 2 minutes. Taste and adjust the seasoning, if necessary and serve the curry hot, with plain rice.

- Serves 4
- Preparation time: 20 minutes
- Cooking time: 50 minutes

2 tablespoons groundnut oil
5 shallots, chopped
2 garlic cloves, crushed
5 cm/2 inch piece of fresh root ginger, grated
2 tablespoons hot curry powder
I teaspoon ground cinnamon
I teaspoon ground cumin
I teaspoon ground coriander
¼ teaspoon ground cardamom
4 curry leaves
I star anise
4 whole cloves
375 g/12 oz sirloin steak, cut into I cm/½ inch strips
300 g/10 oz potatoes, peeled and cut into medium-sized chunks
2 large red chillies, deseeded and finely chopped
½ teaspoon salt
300 ml/½ pint coconut milk
juice of I lime
I teaspoon soft brown sugar

Squid Sambal

I Place the ingredients for the spice paste in a blender or food processor and blend to produce a thick paste. Heat the oil in a large saucepan, add the paste and fry over a moderate heat for 8 minutes, stirring constantly until the paste is cooked and lightly golden.

2 Strain the tamarind pulp through a sieve, pressing it against the sieve to extract as much tamarind flavour as possible. Discard the pulp and add the strained tamarind liquid to the pan with the sugar, paprika and salt. Cook the sambal sauce over a very gentle heat, stirring occasionally, for about 10 minutes.

3 Cut the squid tubes into 2.5 cm/1 inch thick rings and add them and the tentacles to the pan. Increase the heat and cook the squid sambal, stirring constantly, for 5–6 minutes or until the squid is cooked and the sauce is thick. Serve with sliced cucumber and Nasi Lemak (see page 105).

- Serves 4
- Preparation time: 15 minutes
- Cooking time: 25 minutes

3 tablespoons groundnut oil
I tablespoon tamarind pulp soaked in 150 ml/¼ pint boiling water for 10 minutes
1½ teaspoons soft brown sugar
2 teaspoons paprika
½ teaspoon salt
500 g/1 lb small squid with tentacles, cleaned
Spice Paste:
2 large onions, chopped
3 garlic cloves, chopped
I teaspoon dried shrimp paste
1½ tablespoons sambal oelek (hot pepper condiment)
I tablespoon chopped fresh lemon grass

89

Indonesia

Tamarind and peanuts, shrimp paste and coconut milk - many of the ingredients of Indonesian curries are the same as those found in neighbouring Malayisa. The piquancy of the chillies is often increased by the use of sambal oelek, a very hot sauce made from chillies and vinegar. And although the strictest vegetarians might object to the use of shrimp paste, there are many tempting vegetable curries.

Aubergine Petjal

The English translation for this dish is Aubergine and Peanut Curry. This delicious recipe is illustrated on pages 90–91.

1 Rub the salt all over the cubed aubergine and place it in a steamer above a pan of boiling water. Steam the aubergine for about 5 minutes, until it is just tender. Drain and set aside.
2 Heat the oil in a wok, add the shallots and garlic, and fry over a gentle heat, stirring frequently, for 5 minutes, or until softened. Add the shrimp paste and galangal (laos) powder, and fry for a further 3 minutes.
3 Add the coconut milk, tamarind, soy sauce, sambal oelek and sugar. Stir well and simmer gently for 3 minutes. Stir the steamed aubergine into the sauce and cook gently for a further 5 minutes. Add the ground peanuts to the curry and cook gently for 2 minutes.
4 Serve the curry immediately, with plain boiled rice or Nasi Guriah (see page 105).

½ teaspoon salt

750 g/1½ lb aubergines, cut into 2.5 cm/1 inch cubes

3 tablespoons groundnut oil

4 shallots, chopped

2 garlic cloves, crushed

1 teaspoon dried shrimp paste

½ teaspoon galangal (laos) powder

250 ml/8 fl oz coconut milk

1 teaspoon tamarind paste

1 tablespoon dark soy sauce

1 tablespoon sambal oelek (hot pepper condiment)

1 tablespoon palm sugar or soft brown sugar

125 g/4 oz roasted peanuts, coarsely ground

- Serves 6
- Preparation time: about 10 minutes
- Cooking time: 25 minutes

Balinese Duck Curry

It is illustrated on pages 90–91.

1 Place all the ingredients for the spice paste in a blender or food processor and blend to produce a thick paste. Heat the vegetable oil in a wide sauté pan, add the paste and fry over a gentle heat, stirring constantly, for about 3 minutes or until softened and fragrant.
2 Add the duck portions, lemon grass, lime leaves and salt to the pan. Stir to coat the duck evenly in the spice mixture and fry for a further 4 minutes to seal the meat.
3 Add 300 ml/½ pint water, stir well and bring to the boil. Reduce the heat, cover the pan and cook the curry gently, stirring occasionally, for 45 minutes, until the duck is tender.
4 Uncover the pan, stir in the sugar and increase the heat to moderate. Cook the curry, stirring frequently, for a further 30 minutes, until the duck is cooked and the sauce is thick.
5 Skim off any surplus fat from the surface of the curry. Taste and adjust the seasoning if necessary. Serve hot garnished with sliced chillies.

4 tablespoons vegetable oil

1 x 1.5 kg/3 lb oven-ready duck, cut into 4 portions

1 stalk of lemon grass, halved lengthways

4 Kaffir lime leaves, bruised

1 teaspoon salt

2 teaspoons soft brown sugar

2 green chillies, sliced, to garnish

Spice Paste:

8 shallots, chopped

4 garlic cloves, chopped

6 large green chillies, deseeded and chopped

5 cm/2 inch piece of fresh root ginger, chopped

2.5 cm/1 inch piece of fresh galangal, chopped

2 teaspoons turmeric

¼ teaspoon ground black pepper

6 candlenuts or macadamia nuts (optional)

- Serves 4
- Preparation time: 25 minutes
- Cooking time: 1½ hours

Indonesian Fish Curry

1 Wash the mackerel fillets and pat dry on kitchen paper. Cut each fillet into pieces measuring about 7 cm/3 inches x 5 cm/2 inches. Rub the fillets with ½ teaspoon of the salt and the lemon juice. Set aside.

2 Place the remaining salt, onion, garlic, ginger, turmeric, shrimp paste, sambal oelek, lemon grass and coconut milk in a wide sauté pan. Bring to simmering point, then reduce the heat and cook gently for 15 minutes until the sauce has thickened slightly.

3 Strain the tamarind pulp through a sieve, pressing it against the sieve to extract as much tamarind flavour as possible. Discard the pulp and add the strained liquid to the sauce. Stir well and cook gently for a further 5 minutes.

4 Add the mackerel and chopped coriander and cook over a low heat for 6–7 minutes until the fish is cooked.

5 Stir in the grated coconut, cook for 3 minutes or until the coconut has dissolved. Serve garnished with coriander.

750 g/1½ lb mackerel fillets

1 teaspoon salt

juice of ½ lemon

1 large onion, finely chopped

4 garlic cloves, crushed

1 tablespoon grated fresh root ginger

1 teaspoon turmeric

1 teaspoon dried shrimp paste

1 tablespoon sambal oelek (hot pepper condiment)

1 stalk of fresh lemon grass, halved lengthways

300 ml/½ pint coconut milk

1 tablespoon tamarind pulp soaked in 150 ml/¼ pint boiling water for 10 minutes

3 tablespoons chopped fresh coriander

25 g/1 oz creamed coconut, grated finely

a few sprigs of coriander, to garnish

- Serves 6
- Preparation time: 20 minutes, plus 10 minutes soaking time
- Cooking time: 35 minutes

Opor Ayam

The English translation for this dish is Chicken and Coconut Milk Curry.

1 Place all the ingredients for the spice paste in a blender or spice mill and blend to produce a thick paste. Rub the paste over the chicken pieces and place in a non-metallic dish. Cover and marinate for 2 hours.

2 Heat 2 tablespoons of the oil in a sauté pan. Add the onions and fry over a moderate heat, stirring frequently, for 10 minutes or until softened and golden. Remove with a slotted spoon; drain on kitchen paper.

3 Add the remaining oil to the pan and stir in the chicken. Fry over a low heat for 15 minutes, turning occasionally, until pale golden. Remove the chicken from the pan, stir in 300 ml/½ pint of the coconut milk and 300 ml/½ pint water. Add the lemon grass, cinnamon and curry leaves, bring to the boil, then return the chicken to the pan and cook, uncovered, over a low heat for 40 minutes.

4 Stir in the remaining coconut milk and lemon juice, and cook for 10 minutes. Serve hot garnished with the onions.

1 x 2 kg/4 lb chicken, cut into 8 pieces

4 tablespoons vegetable oil

2 onions, thinly sliced

450 ml/¾ pint coconut milk

1 stalk of lemon grass, bruised

5 cm/2 inch cinnamon stick

4 dried curry leaves

1 teaspoon lemon juice

Spice Paste:

4 garlic cloves, crushed

2.5 cm/1 inch piece of fresh root ginger, chopped

2 tablespoons finely chopped Brazil nuts

1 tablespoon ground coriander

2 teaspoons ground cumin

2 teaspoons chopped fresh galangal

1 teaspoon salt

½ teaspoon fennel seeds, crushed

¼ teaspoon ground black pepper

1 tablespoon vegetable oil

- Serves 4
- Preparation time: 20 minutes, plus 2 hours marinating time
- Cooking time: 1 hour 20 minutes

Sayur Kari

Sayur Kari is translated as Vegetable Curry with Fried Beancurd and it is best served immediately with rice. This dish is illustrated opposite.

1 Heat the oil for deep-frying to 180–190°C (350–375°F), or until a cube of bread browns in 30 seconds. Deep-fry the beancurd cubes in batches for about 1 minute, until they are crisp and golden. Remove with a slotted spoon, drain on kitchen paper and set aside.

2 Heat the vegetable oil in saucepan, add the shallots, chillies, garlic, ginger and lemon grass, and fry over a gentle heat, stirring frequently, for 5 minutes, until softened.

3 Add the ground spices, chilli powder and shrimp paste, and fry for a further 1 minute. Stir in the stock and coconut milk. Bring to the boil and add the potatoes. Reduce the heat and cook the potatoes for 6 minutes. Add the beans and cook for a further 8 minutes.

4 Stir in the cabbage, bean sprouts, vermicelli and some salt and cook gently for a further 3 minutes. Stir in the fried beancurd and serve.

- Serves 6
- Preparation time: 20 minutes
- Cooking time: 35 minutes

oil for deep-frying

4 squares of yellow beancurd cut into 2.5 cm/1 inch cubes

2 tablespoons vegetable oil

4 shallots, sliced

2 fresh green chillies, deseeded and sliced

3 garlic cloves, chopped

1 tablespoon finely chopped fresh root ginger

1 stalk of lemon grass, finely chopped

1 tablespoon ground coriander

1 teaspoon ground cumin

1 teaspoon turmeric

1 teaspoon galangal (laos) powder

1 teaspoon chilli powder

1 teaspoon shrimp paste

600 ml/1 pint vegetable stock

400 ml/14 fl oz coconut milk

250 g/8 oz potato, diced

125 g/4 oz green beans, topped, tailed and cut into 1 cm/½ inch lengths

125 g/4 oz white cabbage, shredded finely

75 g/3 oz bean sprouts

25 g/1 oz dried rice vermicelli, soaked in boiling water for 5 minutes, then drained

salt

Indonesian Beef Rendang

This is a classic Indonesian curry. It is very tender and flavoursome due to the long, slow cooking process.

1 Place all the ingredients for the curry paste in a blender or food processor and process to produce a thick paste. Heat the oil in a heavy-based saucepan, add the curry paste and fry over a gentle heat, stirring occasionally, for 5 minutes. Add the beef, turmeric, chilli powder, salt, ground coriander, lemon grass and curry leaves to the pan. Stir well and fry gently for a further 8 minutes.

2 Stir in the coconut milk and strained tamarind liquid. Cook the curry over a low heat, stirring occasionally, for 1½ hours, until the meat is tender and the sauce is thick. Stir in the sugar and cook for a further 2 minutes. Taste and adjust the seasoning if necessary.

3 Serve the beef rendang hot, garnished with toasted coconut and prawn crackers. Plain boiled rice or saffron rice would go well with this curry.

- Serves 6
- Preparation time: 20 minutes
- Cooking time: 1¾ hours

3 tablespoons vegetable oil

750 g/1½ lb rump steak, cut into 2.5 cm/1 inch cubes

1 teaspoon turmeric

1 teaspoon chilli powder

1 teaspoon salt

1 tablespoon ground coriander

10 cm/4 inch piece of fresh lemon grass, halved lengthways

4 curry leaves

150 ml/¼ pint coconut milk

1 tablespoon tamarind pulp soaked in 150 ml/¼ pint boiling water for 10 minutes, then strained

2 teaspoons soft brown sugar

Curry Paste:

2 large onions, chopped

6 garlic cloves, chopped

6 red chillies, deseeded and chopped

2.5 cm/1 inch piece of fresh root ginger, chopped finely

150 ml/¼ pint coconut milk

To garnish:

1½ tablespoons toasted coconut flakes

prawn crackers

Variation

Malaysian Beef Rendang

1 Make a curry paste by blending the following ingredients together in a blender or food processor: 10 dried red chillies, soaked in cold water for 10 minutes, then deseeded and chopped; 10 black peppercorns; 2 teaspoons turmeric; 6 garlic cloves, chopped; 2 large onions, chopped and 2 stalks of lemon grass, finely chopped.

2 Heat 4 tablespoons of groundnut oil in a heavy-based saucepan, add the curry paste and fry over a gentle heat, stirring, for 8 minutes. Add 750 g/1½ lb rump or fillet steak cut into bite-sized pieces and 1 teaspoon of salt and cook, stirring, for a further 3 minutes to seal the meat.

3 Add 600 ml/1 pint coconut milk to the curry a little at a time, allowing it to be absorbed between each addition. Reduce the heat and cook the curry over a gentle heat for about 1 hour, stirring occasionally, until the meat is tender and the sauce is thick.

4 Stir 125 g/4 oz creamed coconut, grated, into the curry and cook over a very low heat for 5 minutes. Stir in the juice of 1 lime and 2 teaspoons caster sugar and cook slowly for a further 10 minutes. Taste and adjust the seasoning if necessary. Serve the curry hot, garnished with 1 tablespoon of toasted desiccated coconut.

- Serves 6
- Preparation time: 20 minutes
- Cooking time: 1½ hours

96

Sayur Lodeh

The English translation for this vegetable dish is Vegetable and Coconut Curry.

1 Heat the oil in a saucepan, add the onion, garlic and chillies, and fry over a moderate heat, stirring occasionally for 7 minutes, until softened and lightly coloured.

2 Add the ground cumin, coriander, curry powder, shrimp paste and lemon grass, and fry for a further 2 minutes. Stir in the tomatoes, stock and coconut milk. Bring the sauce to simmering point and add the pumpkin. Cook for 3 minutes, then add the cabbage and cook for a further 2 minutes. Add the beans, cauliflower and bamboo shoots to the pan, cover and cook over a gentle heat for 10–12 minutes or until all the vegetables are tender.

3 Stir the peanuts and lemon juice into the curry and season to taste with salt. Serve the curry hot, garnished with prawn crackers.

- Serves 4–6
- Preparation time: 30 minutes
- Cooking time: 30 minutes

2 tablespoons vegetable oil

I onion, thinly sliced

3 garlic cloves, crushed

2 red chillies, deseeded and chopped

½ teaspoon ground cumin

½ teaspoon ground coriander

I teaspoon curry powder

I teaspoon dried shrimp paste

I stalk of lemon grass, finely chopped

2 tomatoes, skinned, deseeded and chopped

300 ml/½ pint chicken or vegetable stock

300 ml/½ pint coconut milk

125 g/4 oz diced pumpkin

150 g/5 oz white cabbage, shredded coarsely

150 g/5 oz French beans, topped and tailed, sliced thinly

150 g/5 oz small cauliflower florets

200 g/7 oz canned bamboo shoots, drained

2 tablespoons roasted peanuts, roughly chopped

2 teaspoons lemon juice

salt

10 prawn crackers, to garnish

Pineapple and Coconut Curry

This makes a good accompaniment to beef or chicken curry.

1 Peel the pineapple, taking care to remove all the eyes. Cut the pineapple in half lengthways, cut away and discard the core and cut the flesh into 2.5 cm/1 inch chunks.

2 Heat the oil in a flameproof casserole, add the onion, garlic, cloves and cinnamon stick and fry over a gentle heat, stirring frequently, for about 5 minutes or until softened.

3 Add the ground cardamom, turmeric, cumin, coriander, chilli and salt to the pan, and fry for a further 2 minutes. Add the pineapple chunks and stir well to coat them evenly in the spice mixture.

4 Stir in the coconut milk, stir to mix and bring to the boil, then reduce the heat and cook the curry gently, stirring frequently, for 2–3 minutes or until the pineapple is tender but not mushy and the sauce is very thick. Taste and adjust the seasoning if necessary and serve immediately.

- Serves 6
- Preparation time: about 15 minutes
- Cooking time: 10 minutes

I ripe pineapple

2 tablespoons groundnut oil

I red onion, sliced

2 garlic cloves, crushed

2 whole cloves, bruised

5 cm/2 inch cinnamon stick

¼ teaspoon ground cardamom

½ teaspoon turmeric

2 teaspoons ground cumin

I tablespoon ground coriander

I large fresh red chilli, deseeded and sliced

½ teaspoon salt

75 g/3 oz creamed coconut dissolved in 250 ml/8 fl oz boiling water

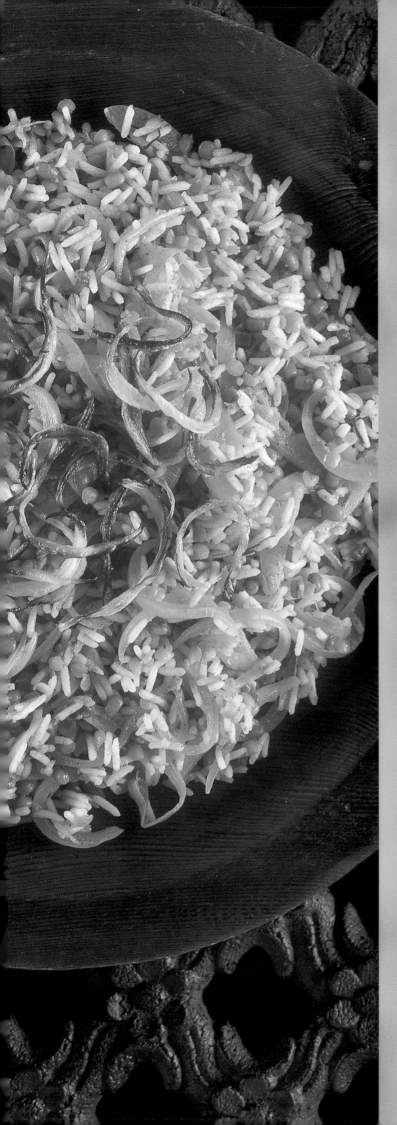

Rice, Breads and Chutneys

No curry is complete without the accompaniment of rice or bread. These may be quite plain, their purpose being to 'mop up' aromatic and tasty sauces, or they may have their own fragrances and flavours – cinnamon or saffron, coconut or sesame seeds – to complement the main dish.

A hot curry calls for the accompaniment of a cooling raita, while fruity chutneys and spicy pickles are perennially popular side dishes.

Kulcha

Kulcha, like naan, is a leavened bread, the difference being that kulcha is grilled and naan is baked. Kulcha is illustrated on pages 98–99.

1 Sift the flour and salt into a large mixing bowl. Sprinkle over the yeast and make a well in the centre. Pour in the measured water and mix well to produce a firm dough.

2 Transfer the dough to a floured work surface and knead for 10 minutes or until it is smooth and elastic.

3 Place the ball of dough in a large greased bowl and cover with oiled clingfilm. Leave the bowl in a warm place for 45 minutes or until the dough has doubled in size.

4 Knock back the dough and add the 2 types of sesame seeds. Work them into the dough, then divide it into 8 equal portions. Roll out each portion to produce a 15 cm/6 inch circle. Make a small cross in the top of each dough circle and brush with the melted butter.

5 Cook the kulcha 2 at a time, under a preheated hot grill, for 3–4 minutes on each side, brushing them with more melted butter when you turn them over. Serve hot.

750 g/1½ lb strong white flour

1 teaspoon salt

15 g/½ oz fast-action dried yeast

450 ml/¾ pint lukewarm water

2 teaspoons black sesame seeds

2 teaspoons white sesame seeds

50 g/2 oz unsalted butter, melted

- Makes 8
- Preparation time: 20 minutes, plus 45 minutes rising time
- Cooking time: 30 minutes

Variation

Onion Kulcha

1 Prepare the kulcha dough as described in the main recipe.

2 Make the onion filling while the dough is proving. Slice 250 g/8 oz onions very thinly and place them in a heavy-based frying pan with 2 tablespoons of vegetable oil, 1 teaspoon soft brown sugar and some salt. Cook them over a gentle heat, stirring frequently, for about 15 minutes or until they are softened and golden. Set aside to cool.

3 Replace the 2 types of sesame seeds used in the main recipe with 1 tablespoon of black onion seeds (kalonji). Divide and roll out the dough as described in the main recipe, then divide the onion filling between the 8 circles and fold the dough over the onions to enclose them. Re-roll the kulcha, slash the tops and brush with 50 g/2 oz unsalted butter, melted. Grill as described in main recipe. Serve hot.

- Makes 8
- Preparation time: 20 minutes, plus 45 minutes rising time
- Cooking time: 35–40 minutes

100

Chapatis

50 g/2 oz wholemeal flour

50 g/2 oz plain flour plus a little more for dusting

½ teaspoon salt

1 Place the wholemeal flour in a bowl. Sift in the 50 g/2 oz plain flour and salt and mix to combine the 2 types of flour.

2 Make a well in the centre of the flour and pour in 75 ml/3 fl oz water. Using a wooden spoon, gradually draw the flour into the well and mix to produce a soft dough.

3 Transfer the dough to a lightly floured surface and knead for about 5 minutes, or until it is smooth and elastic.

4 Divide the dough into 4 equal portions. On a lightly floured surface carefully roll out each portion to produce a thin 15 cm/6 inch circle.

5 Heat a cast-iron frying pan until it is very hot then turn the heat down to low. Cook the chapatis one at a time for 1 minute on each side until golden brown spots appear on the surface of each chapati. Serve the chapatis hot, as an accompaniment to curries.

- Makes 4
- Preparation time: 20 minutes
- Cooking time: about 15 minutes

Variation

Roti

1 Sift together 250 g/8 oz plain flour, ½ teaspoon bicarbonate of soda and ¼ teaspoon salt. Make a well in the centre of the dry ingredients and pour in 75 ml/3 fl oz milk. Using a wooden spoon, gradually draw the flour into the well and mix to produce a stiff dough.

2 Transfer the dough to a floured surface and knead for 4–5 minutes or until it is smooth. Divide the dough into 8 equal portions. Roll each portion into a ball, flatten slightly and place ¼ teaspoon ghee in the centre of each dough ball. Fold the dough over the ghee, knead briefly and leave the dough balls to rest for 30 minutes, covered with a tea towel.

3 On a lightly floured surface roll out each roti to produce a 15 cm/6 inch circle. Brush each roti with a little melted ghee and cook them one at a time on a preheated griddle or in a preheated cast-iron frying pan for 2–3 minutes on each side, until they are cooked and lightly browned on both sides. Serve hot with curries of your choice.

- Makes 8
- Preparation time: 15 minutes plus, 30 minutes resting time
- Cooking time: 40–50 minutes

Sri Lankan Yellow Rice

This delicious recipe is illustrated opposite.

1 Wash the rice in several changes of water and then set it aside in a sieve, to drain.

2 Heat the ghee or oil in a large heavy-based saucepan. Add the onion and garlic, and fry over a medium heat, stirring occasionally, for 5 minutes or until they are lightly golden.

3 Add all the spices to the pan, stir to mix and cook for a further 1 minute. Stir in the rice and salt, and mix so the rice grains are coated in the spicy oil. Cook for 2 minutes.

4 Stir in the coconut milk and stock, bring to the boil, then cover the pan and simmer the rice very gently for 20–25 minutes. (Do not remove the lid during this time.)

5 Lift the lid of the pan and check the rice. It should be cooked and all the liquid should have been absorbed. The spices should have risen to the surface so carefully remove and discard them. Fluff up the rice with a fork and gently stir in the sultanas.

6 Transfer the rice to a warm serving dish and scatter over the flaked almonds. Serve immediately.

375 g/12 oz basmati rice

3 tablespoons ghee or vegetable oil

1 large onion, thinly sliced

2 garlic cloves, finely chopped

6 cloves

6 cardamom pods, bruised

7 cm/3 inch piece of cinnamon stick, bruised

½ teaspoon black peppercorns

10 curry leaves (optional)

10 cm/4 inch stalk of lemon grass, halved lengthways

1 teaspoon turmeric

1 teaspoon salt

600 ml/1 pint thin coconut milk

300 ml/½ pint vegetable stock

50 g/2 oz sultanas

25 g/1 oz toasted flaked almonds

- Serves 6
- Preparation time: 10 minutes
- Cooking time: 35 minutes

Parsee Pilau Rice

This rich rice dish goes particularly well with rich Indian curries like Lamb Dhansak or Chicken Bhuna. It is illustrated on page 103.

1 Heat the ghee in a wide, heavy-based saucepan. Stir in the cardamom pods, cloves, cinnamon stick and peppercorns, and fry over a gentle heat, stirring constantly, for 2 minutes until fragrant. Add the saffron threads and rice to the pan and fry, stirring constantly, for a further minute.

2 Add the salt, orange-flower water, if using, and 600 ml/1 pint water. Stir well to mix. Bring to the boil, then reduce the heat, cover the pan and cook the rice gently for 15 minutes without removing the lid.

3 Remove the pan from the heat and lightly loosen the rice grains with a fork. (All the water should have been absorbed.) Stir the sultanas into the rice, cover the pan with a clean, dry tea towel and allow the rice to cook in its own heat for a further 5 minutes.

4 Just before serving, stir the 2 types of nuts into the rice. Serve hot.

2 tablespoons ghee

6 cardamom pods, bruised

5 whole cloves

7 cm/3 inch piece of cinnamon stick, broken in half

¼ teaspoon black peppercorns, lightly crushed

¼ teaspoon saffron threads

375 g/12 oz basmati rice

¾ teaspoon salt

½ teaspoon orange-flower water (optional)

25 g/1 oz sultanas

25 g/1 oz roasted cashew nuts

25 g/1 oz pistachio nuts

- Serves 4–6
- Preparation time: 5 minutes
- Cooking time: 25 minutes

Nasi Kunyit – Malaysian Glutinous Rice

Glutinous 'sticky' rice is available from oriental grocers. This dish goes well with Nonya curries from Malaysia. It is illustrated on pages 98/9.

1 Place the rice in a sieve and wash it thoroughly under cold water. Drain it and place it in a wide saucepan with 475 ml/16 fl oz water, salt, turmeric, peppercorns and pandanus leaves, if using. Bring to the boil, stirring constantly, then reduce the heat, cover the pan and cook over a low heat for 15 minutes.

2 Place the coconut milk in a saucepan and heat it to just below boiling point. Stir the hot coconut milk into the rice, cover the pan again and cook the rice over a very low heat for a further 10 minutes until all the liquid has been absorbed.

3 Remove the pan from the heat and, working quickly, loosen the rice grains with a fork. Cover the pan with a clean, dry tea towel and allow the rice to cook in its own heat for a further 10–15 minutes. Serve hot garnished with crisply fried shallots.

500 g/1 lb glutinous rice

1½ teaspoons salt

1½ teaspoons turmeric

½ teaspoon whole white peppercorns, crushed lightly

2 pandanus (screwpine) leaves, bruised (optional)

475 ml/16 fl oz coconut milk

2 shallots, thinly sliced and crisply fried, to garnish

- Serves 6–8
- Preparation time: 10 minutes
- Cooking time: 45 minutes

Nasi Guriah – Indonesian Spiced Coconut Rice

1 Place the rice in a sieve and wash it thoroughly under cold water. Drain and place it in a large heavy-based saucepan. Dissolve the creamed coconut in 750 ml/1½ pints boiling water. Add the coconut milk to the rice along with all the remaining ingredients.

2 Bring the rice to the boil and boil, uncovered, over a moderate heat for 8 minutes, stirring frequently, until almost all the liquid is absorbed.

3 Reduce the heat to low, cover the pan with a tightly-fitting lid and cook the rice very gently for a further 10 minutes.

4 Remove the pan from the heat and working quickly, loosen the rice grains with a fork. Cover the pan with a clean, dry tea towel and allow the rice to cook in its own heat for a further 15 minutes. Serve immediately.

375 g/12 oz basmati rice

125 g/4 oz creamed coconut, chopped

7 cm/3 inch piece of lemon grass, halved lengthways

5 cm/2 inch piece of cinnamon stick, broken in half

4 curry leaves

½ teaspoon ground nutmeg

¼ teaspoon ground cloves

1 teaspoon salt

pinch of ground black pepper

- Serves 6
- Preparation time: 5 minutes
- Cooking time: 35 minutes

Variation

Nasi Lemak – Coconut Rice

For a plainer version of the main recipe, omit all the spices – but do not forget to add 1 teaspoon of salt when cooking the rice in the coconut milk.

- Serves 6
- Preparation time: 5 minutes
- Cooking time: 35 minutes

105

Pineapple Chutney

Try this tangy chutney as an unusual alternative to classic mango chutney. It is illustrated opposite.

1 Place the prepared pineapple with all the other ingredients in a heavy-based saucepan. Cook over a moderate heat, stirring constantly, until the sugar has dissolved. Bring the mixture to the boil, then reduce the heat a little and cook on a steady boil for 8–10 minutes, stirring occasionally, until most of the liquid has evaporated and the chutney is thick.

2 Pour the hot chutney into sterilized jars, seal, label and store. Once opened, the chutney will keep well for 3–4 weeks in the refrigerator. Serve with poppadums or as an accompaniment to curries.

1 large, ripe, pineapple, peeled, cored and chopped into small pieces

3 shallots, chopped

1 green chilli, deseeded and finely chopped

1 tablespoon finely chopped fresh root ginger

25 g/1 oz raisins

125 g/4 oz soft brown sugar

125 ml/4 fl oz distilled malt vinegar

¼ teaspoon salt

- Makes about 475 g/15 oz
- Preparation time: 10 minutes
- Cooking time: 15 minutes

Papaya and Coriander Raita

This cooling accompaniment could be made with fresh mango instead of the papaya. It is illustrated on page 107.

I Place all the ingredients in a bowl; mix gently to combine. Taste and adjust the seasoning, adding more lime juice if liked.
2 Cover the raita and leave in the refrigerator for 30 minutes before serving to allow all the flavours to develop. Serve as an accompaniment to curries.

175 g/6 oz natural yogurt
½ ripe papaya, peeled, deseeded and diced
2 tablespoons chopped fresh coriander
½ teaspoon finely grated lime zest
I teaspoon lime juice (or more, according to taste)
salt

- Serves 4
- Preparation time: 10 minutes, plus 30 minutes chilling time

Variations

Cucumber and Mint Raita

This delicious accompaniment is illustrated on page 107.

I Place the following ingredients in a bowl and mix gently to combine: 175 g/6 oz natural yogurt, 75 g/3 oz cucumber, cut into matchsticks, 2 tablespoons chopped fresh mint, a pinch of ground cumin, lemon juice to taste and a little salt.
2 Leave the raita to stand for 30 minutes before serving to allow the flavours to develop.

- Serves 4
- Preparation time: 10 minutes, plus 30 minutes chilling time

Banana and Coconut Raita

I Place the following ingredients in a bowl and mix gently to combine: 175 g/6 oz natural yogurt, 2 small bananas, sliced thinly, 2 tablespoons toasted desiccated coconut, a pinch of chilli powder, lemon juice to taste and a little salt.
2 Taste and adjust the seasoning if necessary. Serve the raita immediately as an accompaniment to curries.

- Serves 4
- Preparation time: 10 minutes

Lentil Biriyani

Nasi Minyak

The English translation for this dish is Fragrant Ghee Rice.

1 Rinse the soaked mung beans thoroughly and place them in a pan of cold water. Bring to the boil, cover the pan and boil rapidly for 10 minutes. Reduce the heat and cook for a further 20–25 minutes until the beans are tender. Drain and set aside.
2 Cook the red lentils and basmati rice in separate pans of salted boiling water for 10 minutes or until cooked. Drain the cooked lentils and the rice and set aside.
3 Heat the ghee in a frying pan, add the onion, garlic, ginger and chillies, and fry over a gentle heat for 5 minutes until softened. Add the coriander, cumin, garam masala and salt, and fry, stirring, for 5 minutes more. Stir in the saffron with its water and cook for 1 minute.
4 Place the mung beans, lentils and rice in a large mixing bowl. Add the cooked onion and spice mixture and stir well.
5 Transfer the rice mixture to a lightly greased ovenproof dish, cover and cook in a preheated oven, 200°C (400°F), Gas Mark 6, for 15–20 minutes to heat it through. Serve the lentil biriyani garnished with crisply fried onions.

- Serves 6
- Preparation time: 20 minutes plus overnight soaking
- Cooking time: 1¼ hours

75 g/3 oz mung beans, soaked in cold water overnight
75 g/3 oz red lentils, washed thoroughly
175 g/6 oz basmati rice
4 tablespoons ghee
2 onions, thinly sliced
4 garlic cloves, crushed
1 tablespoon grated fresh root ginger
1 red chilli, deseeded and finely chopped
1 green chilli, deseeded and finely chopped
2 teaspoons ground coriander
2 teaspoons ground cumin
1 teaspoon garam masala (see page 117)
1 teaspoon salt
½ teaspoon saffron threads soaked in 2 tablespoons boiling water for 10 minutes
½ onion, sliced and crisply fried, to garnish

1 Place the rice in a sieve and wash it thoroughly under cold water. Drain and set aside.
2 Heat the ghee or oil in a saucepan, add the onion, cinnamon, cloves and star anise, and fry over a gentle heat, stirring for 10 minutes or until softened but not coloured.
3 Add the basmati rice, the turmeric and the salt, and cook, stirring constantly, for about 2 minutes. Pour in 600 ml/1 pint water and bring to the boil. Boil, uncovered, over a moderate heat for about 5–8 minutes, stirring frequently until almost all the water is absorbed.
4 Reduce the heat to low, cover the pan with a tightly-fitting lid and cook the rice gently for a further 10 minutes. Remove the pan from the heat and, working quickly, loosen the rice grains with a fork. Cover the pan with a clean dry tea towel and allow the rice to cook in its own heat for a further 10 minutes. Serve hot, garnished with the hard-boiled eggs and fried shallots.

- Serves 4
- Preparation time: 5 minutes
- Cooking time: 40 minutes

375 g/12 oz basmati rice
3 tablespoons ghee or vegetable oil
1 onion, finely chopped
10 cm/4 inch piece of cinnamon stick, broken in half
6 whole cloves
1 star anise
¼ teaspoon turmeric
½ teaspoon salt
To garnish:
2 hard-boiled eggs, quartered
2 shallots, sliced and crisply fried

109

Mango Chutney

The concentrated flavour of dried mangoes makes this a particularly fruity-tasting chutney. It is illustrated opposite.

1 Drain the dried mangoes, reserving 300 ml/½ pint of the soaking liquid and cut the mangoes into 1.5 cm/¾ inch pieces.
2 Place the chilli powder, cardamom pods, cloves, mustard seeds, coriander seeds, peppercorns and cinnamon stick in a large, heavy-based saucepan. Dry-fry the spices over a gentle heat, stirring frequently, for 2–3 minutes until fragrant.
3 Add the reserved mango soaking liquid, the chopped dried and the fresh mango, the garlic, salt and vinegar to the spices. Bring the mixture to the boil, then reduce the heat and simmer gently for 10 minutes, stirring occasionally.
4 Add the sugar and stir over a gentle heat until it has dissolved. Raise the heat and boil the chutney, stirring frequently, until it is thick. This will take about 40 minutes.
5 Ladle the chutney into sterilized jars, seal, label and store for 2–3 months.

250 g/8 oz dried mangoes, soaked covered in cold water overnight

1 teaspoon chilli powder

6 cardamom pods, bruised

3 whole cloves

1 teaspoon black mustard seeds

1 teaspoon coriander seeds, lightly crushed

5 black peppercorns, lightly crushed

1 small cinnamon stick, broken in half

375 g/12 oz fresh mango flesh, cut into 1 cm/½ inch cubes

1 large garlic clove, sliced thinly

½ teaspoon salt

300 ml/½ pint white wine vinegar

375 g/12 oz caster sugar

- Makes about 1 kg/2 lb
- Preparation time: 20 minutes plus overnight soaking
- Cooking time: 55 minutes

Green Bean Sambal

This sambal, illustrated on page 111, makes a good accompaniment to both Indonesian and Malaysian curries.

1 Heat the oil in a frying pan, add the shallots, garlic and shrimp paste, and fry over a low heat, stirring frequently, for 5 minutes until softened.

2 Add the prepared beans, increase the heat to moderate and fry, stirring occasionally, for 8 minutes, until the beans are cooked but not too soft.

3 Stir in the sambal oelek, sugar and a little salt and continue frying the beans for a further minute. Taste and add a little more salt if necessary. Serve the sambal hot.

2 tablespoons vegetable oil

4 shallots, thinly sliced

2 garlic cloves, crushed

½ teaspoon shrimp paste

250 g/8 oz green beans, topped, tailed and sliced thinly on an acute angle

2 teaspoons sambal oelek (hot pepper condiment)

1 teaspoon soft brown sugar

salt

- Serves 4
- Preparation time: 15 minutes
- Cooking time: 15 minutes

Aubergine Pickle

Some Indian grocers sell split mustard seeds, but if these are unavailable, use ordinary mustard seeds instead.

1 Place the cubed aubergine in a colander, sprinkle over the salt and set aside for 30 minutes, to allow the moisture to be drawn out of the aubergine.

2 Heat the oil in a large, heavy-based sauté pan, add the turmeric, cumin, coriander, split mustard seeds and chilli powder, and fry over a gentle heat, stirring constantly, for 3 minutes, until fragrant.

3 Add the ginger, garlic, chillies and vinegar, and stir well. Simmer gently for 10 minutes, stirring occasionally.

4 Add the drained aubergine cubes and the sugar to the pan. Mix well and cook over a moderate heat, stirring occasionally, for 35 minutes, or until the aubergine is very soft and all the flavours are well combined.

5 Ladle the aubergine pickle into sterilized jars, seal and label. This pickle will keep well for 2–3 months.

375 g/12 oz aubergines, cut into 1 cm/½ inch cubes

1 tablespoon salt

75 ml/3 fl oz vegetable oil

1 teaspoon turmeric

1 teaspoon ground cumin

1 teaspoon ground coriander

1 teaspoon split mustard seeds

1 tablespoon chilli powder

5 cm/2 inch piece of fresh root ginger, grated

4 garlic cloves, crushed

4 red chillies, deseeded and thinly sliced

4 green chillies, deseeded and thinly sliced

250 ml/8 fl oz white wine vinegar

90 g/3½ oz soft brown sugar

- Makes about 875 g/1¾ lb
- Preparation time: 20 minutes, plus 30 minutes standing time
- Cooking time: 50 minutes

Serundeng

Serundeng is translated into English as Indonesian Spiced Coconut with Peanuts.

1 Place the peanuts on a baking sheet in a preheated oven, 180°C (350°F), Gas Mark 4, for 25–30 minutes, until they are golden brown. Remove and set aside to cool.

2 Dry-fry the coconut in a heavy-based frying pan over a low heat, stirring constantly, for 2–3 minutes until the coconut is pale golden.

3 Add the remaining ingredients except the sugar and peanuts to the frying pan and fry over a gentle heat, stirring constantly, for a further 3–4 minutes until the coconut is deep golden.

4 Transfer the coconut mixture to a bowl and stir in the sugar and peanuts. Allow the serundeng to cool, then store it in an airtight jar. It will keep well for 3–4 weeks. Serve as an accompaniment to Indonesian curries.

125 g/4 oz raw peanuts with skins

75 g/3 oz desiccated coconut

3 tablespoons dried onion flakes

½ teaspoon salt

½ teaspoon ground coriander

½ teaspoon ground cumin

½ teaspoon chilli powder

¼ teaspoon garlic granules

2 teaspoons soft brown sugar

- Serves 4
- Preparation time: 10 minutes
- Cooking time: 35 minutes

Variation

Bawang Goreng

These crisply fried onions are sprinkled on top of curries and rice dishes in Indonesia. They can be used for any recipe which calls for crisply fried onions as a garnish. Dried onion flakes are available from Asian grocers and supermarkets.

1 Use 50 g/2 oz dried onion flakes for this recipe.

2 Heat some vegetable oil for deep-frying to 180–190°C (350–375°F), or until a cube of bread browns in 30 seconds. Place a quarter of the onion flakes in a metal sieve and lower them into the hot oil. Fry them for a few seconds until they are golden brown. Remove and drain on kitchen paper. Repeat with the remaining onions.

3 Allow the fried onions to cool, then store them in an airtight container. They will keep well for 3–4 weeks.

- Serves 4
- Preparation time: 5 minutes
- Cooking time: 1 minute

Powders
and Pastes

The spice blends that form the basis of
every curry sauce are infinitely variable –
in their native lands the recipes may
differ not only from region to region,
but also from cook to cook. The
following powders and pastes are good
starting points: they are very versatile
and can be stored and used as required.
While it is satisfying to make one's own
pastes and powders, if time is short
there are many good, authentic
equivalents available from Asian grocers
and supermarkets.

Basic Indian Curry Powder

This blend of spices is good for making classic Indian curries. Store it in an airtight container in a dark cupboard and it will keep well for 2–3 months. It is illustrated on pages 114–115.

1 Place the chillies, coriander and cumin seeds, cloves and broken cinnamon stick in a large heavy-based frying pan.

2 Dry-fry the spices over a gentle heat, stirring occasionally for about 5 minutes until they are fragrant, lightly toasted and golden. Tip them into a bowl and allow them to cool.

3 Tip the cooled toasted spices into a spice mill, a blender or into a mortar and crush to a powder. Transfer to a bowl and stir in the turmeric, ginger, cardamom and the fenugreek powder. Store the curry powder in an airtight container in a cool, dark place.

6 dried red chillies

2 tablespoons coriander seeds

2 tablespoons cumin seeds

1 teaspoon whole cloves

15 cm/6 inches of cinnamon stick, broken into 2.5 cm/1 inch pieces

1 tablespoon turmeric

1 tablespoon ground ginger

1 teaspoon ground cardamom

¼ teaspoon fenugreek powder

- Makes about 6 tablespoons
- Preparation time: 5 minutes, plus 5–10 minutes cooling time
- Cooking time: 5 minutes

Variation

Sri Lankan Curry Powder

Sri Lankan curry powders are distinctly different from Indian curry powders as each spice is dark-roasted separately, so giving them a heavily roasted flavour.

1 Dry-roast all the spices separately in a small heavy-based frying pan. Each batch should take about 5 minutes to darken and release its flavour.

2 Allow the roasted spices to cool completely, then place them in a blender, a spice mill or mortar and crush them to produce a powder. Transfer them to a bowl and set aside. Place the dried curry leaves and the seeds from the cardamom pods in the blender and crush them to produce a powder. Add them to the bowl of spices with the chilli powder. Mix well and store the curry powder in an airtight container in a cool, dark place.

10 dried curry leaves

10 cardamom pods

1 tablespoon chilli powder

Dry-roasted Spices:

6 tablespoons coriander seeds

4 tablespoons cumin seeds

4 teaspoons fennel seeds

1 teaspoon whole cloves

7 cm/3 inch piece cinnamon stick, broken

- Makes about 12 tablespoons
- Preparation time: 10–15 minutes
- Cooking time: 25 minutes

116

Madras Curry Paste

This popular paste is illustrated on pages 114–115.

1 Place the ground coriander, cumin, turmeric, chilli powder, salt and pepper in a large bowl. Add the garlic, the ginger and vinegar, and mix well to produce a thick paste.

2 Heat the oil in a heavy-based frying pan, add the paste and cook it over a gentle heat, stirring constantly, for 5 minutes until the curry paste is cooked and the oil begins to separate from the spices.

3 Allow the curry paste to cool, then store it in an airtight jar in the refrigerator. Use as required.

- Makes about 12 tablespoons
- Preparation time: 10 minutes
- Cooking time: 5 minutes

6 tablespoons ground coriander

3 tablespoons ground cumin

1 tablespoon turmeric

1 tablespoon chilli powder

2 teaspoons salt

2 teaspoons ground black pepper

6 garlic cloves, crushed

5 cm/2 inch piece of fresh root ginger, grated

6 tablespoons distilled malt vinegar

150 ml/¼ pint groundnut oil

Garam Masala

1 Dry-roast each of the whole spices separately in a heavy-based frying pan until they are fragrant but not too dark. The coriander seeds, black peppercorns and cinnamon sticks will take about 3 minutes to roast. The cumin seeds, whole cloves and mace blades will need about 2 minutes each.

2 As each spice is roasted, tip it into a bowl and allow them to cool. Place the roasted spices in a blender, a spice mill or mortar and crush them to produce a fine powder. Transfer the blended spices to a bowl and stir in the ground cardamom and nutmeg.

3 Store the garam masala in an airtight jar in a cool dark place. Use as required. It will keep well for 2–3 months.

- Makes about 8 tablespoons
- Preparation time: 5 minutes
- Cooking time: 15 minutes

3 tablespoons coriander seeds

1½ tablespoons cumin seeds

1 tablespoon black peppercorns

1 teaspoon whole cloves

3 x 5 cm/2 inch pieces of cinnamon stick

1 teaspoon mace blades

1 teaspoon ground cardamom

½ teaspoon ground nutmeg

117

Thai Red Curry Paste

The hotness of this paste depends on the heat of the chillies used. If a really hot curry paste is required, include a few of the seeds from the chillies. It is illustrated on pages 114–115.

1 Place the ingredients except the groundnut oil in a blender or food processor and blend to produce a smooth, thick paste. Alternatively, crush the ingredients in a large mortar.

2 Heat the oil in a heavy-based frying pan, add the curry paste and fry over a gentle heat, stirring, for about 5 minutes until the curry paste is fragrant.

3 Leave the curry paste to cool completely and store in an airtight jar in the refrigerator. Use as required. The paste will keep for about 2–3 weeks.

- Makes about 10 tablespoons
- Preparation time: 25 minutes
- Cooking time: 5 minutes

2 tablespoons chopped fresh coriander

2 tablespoons ground coriander

1 tablespoon ground cumin

1 teaspoon turmeric

1 teaspoon black peppercorns

1 teaspoon salt

2 teaspoons shrimp paste

2 stalks of lemon grass, chopped finely

4 garlic cloves, chopped finely

10 large red chillies, deseeded and chopped finely

5 cm/2 inch piece of fresh galangal, chopped finely

3 tablespoons groundnut oil

Variation

Thai Green Curry Paste

As with the Thai red curry paste, the addition of the seeds from the chillies will produce a hotter paste.

1 Place all the ingredients in a blender or food processor and blend to produce a smooth, thick paste. Alternatively, crush all the ingredients in a mortar.

2 Transfer the prepared curry paste to an airtight jar and store in the refrigerator. Use as required. The paste will keep for 2–3 weeks.

- Makes about 10 tablespoons
- Preparation time: 25 minutes

10 large green chillies, deseeded and chopped

8 garlic cloves, chopped

2 stalks of lemon grass, chopped

4 large Kaffir lime leaves, chopped

2 shallots, chopped

3 tablespoons chopped fresh coriander

1 tablespoon chopped fresh root ginger

2 teaspoons ground coriander

1 teaspoon ground cumin

1 teaspoon crushed black peppercorns

2 teaspoons shrimp paste

juice of ½ lime

118

Glossary

Asian Fishcake

This is a compressed fresh fishcake which is sold in squares in Chinese and Thai shops. It can be stored in the refrigerator for 1–2 days, and is usually sliced thinly before use. Fish balls have a similar flavour and texture and can be used if fishcake is unavailable.

Banana leaves

In South East Asia and southern India, banana leaves are sometimes used as containers to steam food. They impart a delicate flavour to the steamed food, but if they are unavailable, squares of lightly oiled foil or buttered greaseproof paper can be used instead.

Basil

– see Thai basil

Beancurd

Beancurd or tofu is a product of soya beans; it is high in vitamins and minerals and is an excellent source of protein in a vegetarian diet. Pressed beancurd (ordinary tofu) is sold in blocks. It is available in large supermarkets, Asian shops and health food shops. Yellow beancurd is a light-textured tofu, available from Chinese and Thai shops. It is sold in small squares and is normally deep-fried for use in cooking.

Black Onion Seeds

– see Kalonji

Bok choy/pak choy

This is a leafy green vegetable, one of many types found in Asia. It is available in larger supermarkets and in Chinese shops. Spring greens make an adequate substitute.

Candlenuts

These are cream-coloured, waxy nuts which have a thickening effect when added to curries. Candlenuts are available from Asian shops but can be difficult to find. Macadamia nuts or Brazil nuts can be used as a substitute.

Cardamom

There are 3 types of cardamom pods: white, green and black. The white and green types are most commonly used in cooking. Both have parchment-like skins which encase lots of aromatic black seeds. The white pods have been bleached so they are less flavoursome. Black cardamoms have fibrous skins and an earthy flavour.

Cardamom can be used to flavour curries in 3 ways. If the whole pod is called for, 'bruise' or lightly crush it to release the aroma before adding it to the dish. If cardamom seeds are suggested, they will be far more aromatic if they are removed from the pods just before use, although they can be bought in packets form Indian grocers. Ground cardamom is also sold in packets, although again it is more fragrant if freshly prepared by grinding cardamom seeds to a powder in a spice mill or mortar.

Cellophane Noodles

– see Noodles

Chutneys (various)

These are usually sweet and spicy and are made from fruits, mango being the most popular. They are delicious served with Indian curries as they offset the spiciness.

Chillies

Curries are only truly 'hot' if chillies are used in the recipe, so it is perfectly possible to make a mild curry simply by leaving out the chillies. Although chilli peppers were unknown in Asia before the 16th century, when the Portuguese introduced them from the New World, each Asian country now grows its own varieties of chilli. There are many varieties that, unless you know exactly which sort you are buying, it is best to use with care, otherwise you may end with an inedibly 'hot' curry. Some chillies are always sold fresh and green, other varieties are usually red.

Jalapeño chillies are very hot, shorter and wider than most chillies, with a smooth surface. They may be red or green and are available fresh, canned or pickled.

Red chillies may be dried and sold whole, flaked or ground into a powder. (Some brands of chilli powder include other spices such as cumin, while cayenne pepper, made from a particular variety of hot chilli, can be used wherever chilli powder is called for – chilli paste, chilli sauce and sambal oelek (see page 124) are made to slightly different recipes in each country, but are more or less interchangeable. Sweet chilli sauce is a sweeter, slightly milder condiment, available from Chinese shops.

Coconut milk

This is not the watery liquid from fresh coconuts, but has to be made from shredded coconut flesh, blended with water. Luckily, unsweetened coconut milk is sold in cans in most supermarkets and Asian shops. Coconut milk powder is also available; it needs to be mixed with water (according to the packet instructions) to produce coconut milk, and can be made thicker or thinner with less or more water.

Creamed Coconut

This is a very rich block of concentrated coconut. It needs to be diluted with boiling water to produce coconut milk, and the proportions of creamed coconut to water will provide thicker or thinner water.

Coriander

Fresh coriander is a favourite herb in all Asian countries; it has a unique, delicate flavour and its bright, fresh green colour adds the perfect finishing touch to curries. Supermarkets sell fresh coriander in small packets, but the most economical way of buying it is in the large bunches available from Asian grocers. Stand the whole bunch of coriander leaves in a jug or bowl of cold water, cover with a polythene bag and store in the refrigerator for up to 1 week. Coriander seeds are the spherical, beige-brown seeds of the coriander plant. They are sometimes used whole, sometimes crushed to a powder, as ground coriander. Ground coriander should be bought in small quantities, as it loses its flavour very quickly if stored for any length of time. Always keep it in an airtight container in a cool, dark place.

Cumin

Cumin seeds are narrow, shaped like caraway seeds, and come in white (actually a beige colour) and black varieties. The ordinary white cumin seeds are readily available in supermarkets; the black variety is considered to have a finer flavour and is therefore more expensive, but it is more difficult to find – look for it in Indian grocers, or substitute white cumin. Ground cumin is widely available.

Curry Leaves

These glossy green leaves are southern Indian in origin and are widely used in curries and rice dishes all over Asia. They are available fresh or dried from Indian shops. Fresh curry leaves can be frozen and used as required.

Curry Paste

These are blends of chillies, herbs and spices which are then used as the basis of a curry. Different blends produce different flavours. Curry pastes are very popular in Thai cooking. As they contain fresh ingredients, they need to be refrigerated and used as required.

Curry Powder

These are dry blends of spices and chillies. Different blends and roasting times produce different types of curry powder e. g. Sri Lankan curry powder is a darker blend than Indian curry powder and has a more 'roasted' flavour.

Dhana Jeera Powder

A spice mixture made up of ground roasted coriander and cumin. The proportion of coriander is greater than cumin – a standard mix would be 2 parts coriander to 1 part cumin.

Fennel Seeds

Fennel seeds have an aniseed flavour and are used in many types of curry from vegetarian to seafood. They are small, oval green seeds.

120

Fenugreek

Fenugreek seeds are hard, flat yellow seeds which produce a slightly bitter taste. Fenugreek powder is more commonly used but either type should be used sparingly.

Fish Sauce

This strong-smelling, clear, brown liquid is called Nam Pla in Thailand and Nuoc-Mam in Vietnam. It is made from salted fish and is rich in protein and B vitamins. It has a salty flavour and is used as a seasoning like soy sauce. Although it is milder than soy sauce, it adds a subtle but distinctive flavour to the curries of Thailand and Indochina.

Galangal

Fresh galangal looks similar to root ginger but has a thinner skin, which is cream-coloured and tinged with pink; the skin is usually peeled away and discarded. The flavour is similar to ginger but not so hot, with a slightly citrus taste. Galangal comes in two varieties: lesser (Kanchur) and greater (Laos). Laos is preferred and is the type available in Europe, in Chinese and Thai shops. Ground galangal (Laos powder) is another way of using the plant.

Garam Masala

Garam masala, meaning 'hot spices', is a mixture of highly aromatic spices such as cardamom seeds, black peppercorns, cloves, cumin seeds and nutmeg. The name refers to the fact that these spices are supposed to 'heat' the body. Garam masala is used very widely in northern Indian cooking and there is no standard mixture – each household has its own recipe. My version is on page 117. Alternatively, garam masala can be bought ready-made from Asian shops and some supermarkets. It is often added towards the end of cooking and is used sparingly.

Ghee

Ghee is Indian clarified butter; it gives a rich, nutty taste to Indian curries and rice dishes and is also used in Sri Lanka. Because it is so well, clarified it can be kept for 2–3 months in the refrigerator. Ghee is available from Indian shops and is sold in tins.

Glutinous Rice

Glutinous rice has thick, short grains and looks similar to pudding rice. When cooked, the grains clump together in a sticky mass, hence its name. It is especially popular in Thai and Malaysian 'Nonya' cookery. It can be served as an accompaniment to curries or as a dessert with coconut milk and sugar.

Jalapeño chillies

– see Chillies

Kaffir Lime Leaves

These glossy, dark green leaves are particularly popular in Thai cooking, to which they impart an aromatic citrus flavour. They are available from Chinese and Thai shops, either fresh, frozen or dried. Fresh Kaffir lime leaves can also be frozen at home. The dried lime leaves need to be soaked in warm water to soften them before use. If Kaffir lime leaves are unavailable, strips of lime peel can be used to give a similar flavour.

Kalonji/nigella seeds/black onion seeds

These are small, black, teardrop-shaped seeds that impart an earthy, peppery aroma. Kalonji are widely used in fish curries and in northern Indian breads and can be bought from Indian shops.

Korma Curry Powder

This is a very mild curry powder as it contains little or no chilli, but includes coriander, cumin, mustard seeds, fenugreek and bay leaves.

Lemon Grass

This long, slim, citrus-flavoured bulb is a favourite ingredient in Thailand, Malaysia and Indonesia. It is available from greengrocers, Chinese and Thai shops and supermarkets. Whole bulbs can be bruised and added to curries or, if the recipe calls for chopped lemon grass, first cut off the root tip and peel away the tough outer layers, then finely chop the inner layers.

Mace Blades

'Blades' of mace form a net-like casing on the outside of whole nutmegs. They are very brittle and can easily be ground. The flavour is similar to nutmeg, with a medicinal aroma. Mace is always used sparingly as it is very strong.

121

Masoor dhal

This is the Indian name for red split lentils or orange lentils. They should be thoroughly rinsed and any impurities removed, but do not need soaking before cooking.

Moong dhal

This is the Indian name for split mung beans that have had their husks removed, leaving a yellow or white split bean.

Mung beans

Whole mung beans are small and round with an olive-green skin and a delicate, sweetish flavour. As they are small they cook very quickly and do not need to be soaked beforehand if time is short. Bean sprouts are sprouted mung beans.

Mustard seeds

There are 2 types: the larger, more commonly available yellow mustard seeds and the smaller black mustard seeds which are actually dark reddish brown. Both impart a delicious, nutty flavour to Indian dishes and are more or less interchangeable, although the black ones have a finer taste. Buy them from Indian grocers or some supermarkets.

Mustard oil

This oil, made from mustard seeds, has a pungent taste when raw, but when heated it becomes quite sweet. It is often used in Indian cooking, and is available from Indian shops and some delicatessens.

Noodles

Many types of noodles are used in Asian cooking, although they are rare in India. Some are broad and flat, like Italian tagliatelle, others have the sturdy string-like form of spaghetti, some are very thin and wiry. They may be made from wheat flour, with or without eggs, or from rice or other starches. Cellophane noodles, also called 'glass' or mung bean noodles, are made from the starch of mung beans. They are translucent and are sold dry: they need to be soaked in warm water before use. Thin rice noodles (rice vermicelli) can be used instead of cellophane noodles. A variety of fresh and dried noodles are available from Asian shops.

Orange-flower water

This fragrant, clear liquid flavouring imparts a sweet, citrus aroma to rice dishes and desserts. It is sold in bottles in large supermarkets and in Indian shops.

Palm sugar

Palm sugar comes from the sap of the coconut flower and has a rich, caramelized flavour. It is sold in brown cylindrical blocks in Thai shops. Soft brown sugar makes a satisfactory substitute.

Pandanus/screwpine leaves

Pandanus or screwpine leaves are used in Thai, Malaysian and Indonesian cooking and impart a fragrant, musky flavour to rice dishes and desserts. The leaves need to be torn or bruised to release the fragrance. They are available from Asian greengrocers.

Saffron

One of the world's most expensive spices, saffron threads are the dried stigmas of a particular species of crocus flower, grown in Kashmir in northern India. Saffron adds a unique aroma and yellow colour to rice dishes and curries. Turmeric may be used as a substitute – it will give the colour but not the same flavour.

Sambal oelek (hot pepper condiment)

An Indonesian sauce made with crushed red chillies, salt and vinegar. It is available in jars from Chinese shops.

Sesame seeds

Creamy-white, hulled sesame seeds are the most widely available; sesame seeds are also sold unhulled, when they have a dull beige appearance. Another variety is jet black. All 3 types of sesame seeds are used to give a sweetish, nutty flavour to Indian breads and other dishes.

Shrimp paste

Malaysia, Indonesia and other Asian countries each have their own versions of this very strong-smelling, pungent paste made from shrimps or small fish. Only a small amount is needed to add a salty, fishy taste to curries. It is available from Asian shops, either in jars, or as blocks of dried shrimp paste (sometimes known as belecan or blachan).

Star anise

This is the star-shaped seed pod of a small evergreen plant which grows in south-western China. It has an aniseed-like aroma and is used with rice. It is also one of the spices in Chinese 5-spice powder and is available from supermarkets.

Tamarind

Tamarind is the fruit of the tamarind tree; it is most commonly available as sticky, dark brown blocks of tamarind pulp, in which the fresh tamarind has been removed from its pods and compressed. To extract the sour, slightly acidic flavour, the pulp must be mixed with hot water and then strained (individual recipes give more details). It is available from Asian shops and keeps well in the refrigerator for several months. Concentrated tamarind paste is sold in jars – it is a quick way of incorporating the flavour of tamarind, simply by adding a spoonful or so, as described in more detail in individual recipes.

Thai red and Thai green curry paste

These are the 2 curry pastes most commonly used in Thai cooking. One paste is made with red chillies and various herbs and spices and the other with green chillies and a different blend of herbs and spices. Both are equally fiery, even though the green one looks milder.

Thai basil

Sometimes known as holy basil, this is an Asian variety of the herb sweet basil. It has small green leaves and purple stems and flowers. Thai basil adds a lovely mix of basil and aniseed flavours when used in cooking. It can be found in Chinese and Thai shops, or alternatively the more widely available sweet basil can be substituted.

Turmeric

Turmeric is most commonly sold in its powdered form. Quality can be judged by its colour – the deeper the colour the better the spice. It has a bitter, musky flavour and is an essential ingredient in nearly all Indian curries. It is also used for colouring and flavouring rice dishes.

Fresh turmeric looks like a smaller version of its cousin, ginger, but with an orange-yellow colour. In South-East Asia it is sliced or chopped and added to dishes.

Yellow bean sauce

A flavoursome, salty-tasting sauce made from soya beans. It is used in Thai cooking and is available in jars or bottles, from Chinese and Thai shops.

Index

125